THE CAMBRIDGE BIBLE COMMENTARY

NEW ENGLISH BIBLE

GENERAL EDITORS

P. R. ACKROYD, A. R. C. LEANEY, J. W. PACKER

ROMANS

THE CAMBRIDGE BIBLE COMMENTARY

THE LETTER OF PAUL
TO THE
ROMANS

COMMENTARY BY

ERNEST BEST

*Lecturer in Biblical Literature and Theology
St Mary's College, St Andrews*

CAMBRIDGE

AT THE UNIVERSITY PRESS

1967

Published by the Syndics of the Cambridge University Press
Bentley House, 200 Euston Road, London, N.W.1
American Branch: 32 East 57th Street, New York, N.Y. 10022

Library of Congress Catalogue Card Number: 66-24289

Printed in Great Britain
at the University Printing House, Cambridge
(Brooke Crutchley, University Printer)

GENERAL EDITORS' PREFACE

The aim of this series is to provide the text of the New English Bible closely linked to a commentary in which the results of modern scholarship are made available to the general reader. Teachers and young people preparing for such examinations as the General Certificate of Education at Ordinary or Advanced Level in Britain and similar qualifications elsewhere have been especially kept in mind. The commentators have been asked to assume no specialized theological knowledge, and no knowledge of Greek and Hebrew. Bare references to other literature and multiple references to other parts of the Bible have been avoided. Actual quotations have been given as often as possible.

Within these quite severe limits each commentator will attempt to set out the main findings of recent New Testament scholarship, and to describe the historical background to the text. The main theological content of the New Testament will also be critically discussed.

Much attention has been given to the form of the volumes. The aim is to produce books each of which will be read consecutively from first to last page. The introductory material leads naturally into the text, which itself leads into the alternating sections of commentary.

The series is prefaced by a volume—*Understanding the New Testament*—which outlines the larger historical background, says something about the growth and transmission of the text, and answers the question 'Why should we study the New Testament?' Another volume—*New Testament Illustrations*—contains maps, diagrams, and photographs.

P. R. A.

A. R. C. L.

J. W. P.

EDITOR'S PREFACE

I wish to thank the General Editors for their exceedingly helpful comments during the preparation of this commentary, my wife for typing the manuscripts and assisting in the correction of the proofs, and the Cambridge University Press for their usual excellent work. Any success I may have achieved in clarifying Paul's thought comes from years of practice in attempting to explain Scripture to the congregations of Caledon and Minterburn when I was their minister.

E. B.

CONTENTS

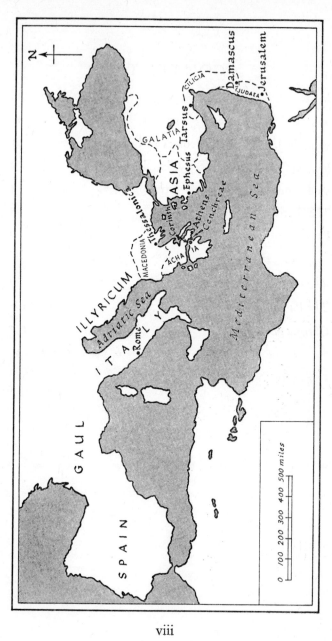

N

GAUL

ILLYRICUM

Adriatic Sea

ITALY

Rome

SPAIN

MACEDONIA
Thessalonica

ACHA

IA

Corinth

Athens
Cenchreae

ASIA

Ephesus

GALATIA

Tarsus

CILICIA

Damascus

JUDAEA

Jerusalem

Mediterranean Sea

0 100 200 300 400 500 miles

viii

THE LETTER OF PAUL TO THE

ROMANS

✳ ✳ ✳ ✳ ✳ ✳ ✳ ✳ ✳ ✳ ✳ ✳ ✳

PAUL, THE JEWISH RABBI, BECOMES A CHRISTIAN

Paul was born in Tarsus, the capital of the Roman province of
Cilicia (in modern Turkey). His family were Jewish and very
strict followers of their faith. He would therefore not have been
educated in the ordinary schools of the city but in the school
attached to the Jewish Synagogue, the centre of Jewish worship
and life. His separate education would have made him very
much aware of the special nature of his religion; this feeling
would have been intensified when he was sent to Jerusalem to
complete his education. There he trained to be a Rabbi, a
teacher whose responsibility it was to understand and expound
to others the details of the Jewish way of life as laid down in their
Law—and this Law covered every aspect of life, religious, ethical, civil (see the note on 'The Law' on pp. 26–28). In this he
was taught by Gamaliel, one of the greatest Rabbis of the
period. Paul devoted himself entirely to the training and became a fanatical Jew and upholder of Jewish ways.

Either during or just after he had finished this training he became aware of the Christians and their preaching, though it is
very unlikely that he ever saw or heard Jesus himself. The Jews
had long been expecting that God would send them a deliverer
to free them from their enemies. They called this deliverer
'Messiah' (the word 'Messiah' is Hebrew and the word 'Christ'
is its Greek translation; both mean 'anointed'). The Christians
proclaimed that Jesus, whom the Romans had executed at the
instigation of the Jews, was this Messiah. This preaching
brought against them the weight of Jewish opinion, and, when
they persisted in it, soon led to their persecution. Paul joined in

I

this persecution; he tells us, 'savagely I persecuted the church of God, and tried to destroy it' (Gal. 1:13).

It was while journeying to Damascus to extend this persecution that Paul had the marvellous experience by which he became a Christian (Acts 9:1–22; cf. Acts 22:3–16; 26:12–18). He does not himself describe it in detail in any of his letters. He does however speak of himself as 'called' through the grace of God (Gal. 1:15) and says, 'Did I not see Jesus our Lord?' (1 Cor. 9:1). Just as the early disciples believed that Jesus appeared to them after his resurrection, so that they were convinced he was alive again, so Paul also believed that in his experience he saw Jesus alive—'he appeared even to me' (1 Cor. 15:8). Fully assured now that the Jesus who had died on the cross was living, he was also certain that he was the Jewish Messiah, and began to preach this message.

JEWS AND GENTILES IN THE EARLY CHURCH

We do not know what happened to Paul in the early years following his conversion to Christianity; when we hear of him again many years later it is as a Christian missionary preaching the Gospel to non-Jews. He had become convinced not only that God had chosen him to be a missionary of Christ but also that his mission was to be specially directed to those who were not Jews. Jesus had been a Jew and had lived and worked in Palestine, the Jewish homeland. The disciples he chose while on earth had all been men of his own race—Jews. It was only natural, when after his death and resurrection they began to preach about him, that they should limit their preaching to fellow Jews. The Jews believed that they themselves had been chosen to be God's people in a very special way. God had freed them from slavery in Egypt and, under Moses as their leader, had brought them to their Promised Land, Palestine; he had laid down for them an elaborate system of sacrifices and worship to be carried out in the temple at Jerusalem; he had given them a detailed code of laws to guide their activities; when they had opposed his will for them and rebelled against him he had sent the prophets to recall them to his ways; finally he had promised to them the Messiah. It was reasonable to expect that the followers of the Messiah should be Jews and that if anyone who was not a Jew wished to become a Christian then he should also become a Jew, i.e. take up Jewish ways, including circumcision. Since many of the people of the ancient world had become Jews, attracted by the simplicity and straightforwardness of Jewish life and worship, this did not seem an unreasonable demand. Christianity would then have been a kind of extension of Judaism, adding to the latter some new beliefs, such as that Jesus was the Messiah, and some extra religious practices, such as the observance of the Lord's Supper.

Although Paul had not himself been the first to preach to the Gentiles this became the central activity of his life. It naturally caused a tremendous upheaval among the early Christians. For a time there was a grave danger that the Church would be split in two—into a section of those who had all been originally Jews, and into a section the great majority of whom had been originally Gentiles; and the Jewish section would hardly have recognized the other as being truly Christian. Had the split ever taken place, Paul, though born a Jew, would undoubtedly have cast in his lot with the latter, largely Gentile group. However, almost entirely through his efforts, the split never occurred, and the early church learned to accept Gentiles with Jews as equal members of their community; but for many years the possibility of a split remained and Paul vigorously defended the acceptance of non-Jews into the Christian church. As we shall see when we read through his letter to the Romans, this dispute colours and largely shapes what he writes. Unlike Jesus' first disciples who had all been ordinary men and women, Paul brought to the discussion a mind trained in all the intricacies of Jewish law. He grasped that if the law, the Jewish way of life and the Old Testament were properly understood, then the way was indicated in them for the introduction of Gentiles into the church. So arguing, he was led to a much deeper understanding of the very nature of what being a Christian meant.

PAUL AS MISSIONARY AND LETTER-WRITER

But Paul was not primarily a controversialist arguing the principle that Gentiles should be admitted into the church on equal terms with Jews; he was above all concerned to see that they actually came in. So he travelled widely, preaching to Jews and Gentiles that Jesus was both the Jewish Messiah and the deliverer for the whole world. His travels took him round the great cities of the eastern Mediterranean and he founded churches in many of them, e.g. Corinth, Ephesus. Normally he began his work by going to the Jewish community in the town to which he had come. Since he was a fellow Jew and a trained Rabbi they would give him a hearing; but when, as almost invariably happened, they as a group rejected his argument that Jesus who had been crucified was their Messiah, he would widen his preaching to take in the Gentiles. Thus a Christian community would come into existence in each town, containing a number of Jewish Christians but largely Gentile in its make-up. He moved from place to place, staying as long as it took him to establish the community on sound foundations or until persecution excluded him.

When, moreover, he had established one church and moved on to work in another area, he did not forget the first community. Many of the letters which he wrote were sent back to these young churches, to help them deal with their difficulties and to bring them to a fuller understanding of the Gospel he had preached to them, so that they should live by it more truly. However the letter that we are about to read was written to a church which he had neither founded nor visited.

Many scholars doubt if Paul wrote all the letters which bear his name in our New Testament. In many editions the letter to the Hebrews is attributed to Paul, but there are no scholars to-day who hold that Paul wrote this letter; it is not attributed to him in the New English Bible. However there is no doubt that he wrote Romans. Indeed Romans, with the two letters to the

4

Corinthian church and the letter to the Galatians, are used as the touchstone by which the others are judged to see if they reveal the same mind behind them.

THE CHURCH IN ROME

The letter is addressed to the Christians in Rome. Paul did not establish this church; no one today knows how it came into existence. There were other Christian missionaries as well as Paul who were active in founding churches, but it is very probable that if the church at Rome had been founded by some such leader Paul would have referred to him in the letter; he does not do this. Sometimes it is said that it was founded by Peter, one of the original disciples of Jesus; but there is nothing in the New Testament that suggests that Peter had ever been in Rome in the period before Paul wrote the letter, and there is a great deal of evidence to show that Peter was a leader of the church in Palestine until at least shortly before its writing and long after the beginning of Christianity in Rome. A long-standing and probably true tradition does hold that Peter and Paul both suffered martyrdom in Rome; so Peter must have come to Rome after this letter was written.

How, then, did the Roman church begin? The Roman historian Suetonius tells us that the Emperor Claudius (A.D. 41–54) expelled the Jews from Rome about A.D. 50 in consequence of rioting over a man named Chrestus. Suetonius, or the reports on which he depended, probably got the name wrong and the rioting was over Christus, i.e. Christ. Some Jews must have been attacking those who were advocating the claims of Jesus to be the Christ or Messiah. Acts 18 : 1–2 tells us about two Jewish Christians, Aquila and his wife Priscilla, who had been forced to leave Rome when the Emperor expelled the Jews. When Nero became Emperor the Jews were allowed to return to the city (A.D. 54); presumably the Jewish Christians returned then also. It is not known whether Gentile Christians had also been forced to leave. The church must thus have been in existence for a few years before Paul wrote. Since Rome was the capital of the ancient world there was a continual flow of people into and out of it on public and private business. Its large Jewish colony would have continually been in touch with Palestine, and Jewish Christians who travelled to Rome would naturally have begun to tell their fellow Jews that the Messiah had come and was Jesus. A Christian community thus established would have grown as other Christians whose business brought them to Rome joined it. If it began in the Jewish colony in Rome it certainly was not limited to Jews; the very fact that in the letter Paul deals with the relationship of Jewish and Gentile Christians shows that it was a church that contained both.

Though at the time of writing Paul has not yet visited Rome, he is hoping to come. He plans to stay a short time and then to go on farther west into areas like Spain where the Gospel has not yet been preached (15:23); for this journey Rome would be his natural base of operations. However, before he comes he intends to go to Jerusalem with a collection of money which he has gathered in his churches for the poor of the Christian community in that city (15:25). Though Paul eventually came to Rome, it was not in the way he planned. When he arrived in Jerusalem he was arrested and falsely accused of stirring up trouble; to escape his enemies he was forced to exercise his rights as a Roman citizen by appealing to the Emperor in Rome. To that city his case was then transferred and he himself sent as a prisoner. The story is told in Acts 21–28.

PAUL'S REASON FOR WRITING

It was in order to prepare the way for the visit he planned that Paul wrote his letter to the Christians in Rome. As we have seen, the early church was almost split by the controversy over the admission of Gentiles; in the controversy Paul himself had been the chief protagonist on behalf of the Gentiles. The church at Rome consisted of both Jews and Gentiles; misleading reports of the views that Paul held may well have been circulating;

6

Paul therefore writes to prepare them for his visit by setting down clearly what he believes to be the truth in the matter. He had already done this at least once before, in his letter to the Galatians. That letter had, however, been written in the full heat of the controversy when no one could have predicted in what way it would end. By the time of Romans it is quite clear that Paul's view had triumphed; almost everywhere Gentile Christians are being accepted into the church on the same terms as Jewish Christians and are not expected to take on themselves obedience to the ceremonial requirements of the Jewish law— the principal requirement was circumcision. With victory practically attained, Paul now sets down in a more reflective manner the underlying principles which led him to contest the issue.

We do not have in this letter a full and rounded exposition of what Paul took Christianity to be. There are many things which he merely mentions in passing, e.g. baptism (6:1–11), assuming that his Roman readers will already know what needs to be known (and what was common knowledge in the early church) about this rite of admission to the church. There are matters on which he does not touch at all; the fact that he does not mention the Lord's Supper should not lead us to believe that it was not celebrated in Rome. In any letter there are always many things which the writer and the reader to whom it is initially addressed will have in common, and for that reason the writer does not explicitly mention them. He may allude to them in passing; when an outsider comes on the letter, this makes it difficult to understand; that is why Paul's meaning sometimes escapes us. Because this is a genuine letter and not a theological treatise it is not a comprehensive account of the nature of Christianity.

Yet because Paul is dealing with an issue of great importance he is compelled to delve to the very heart of Christianity to find a full and satisfying answer. He had the kind of mind that was never satisfied with superficialities; had he been dealing with another question of equal importance he would doubtless have written an entirely different letter, but he would still have dealt with the fundamentals of Christian faith. In this letter, then, we see the greatest of Christian thinkers taking up a particular problem and, in explaining it, laying bare what Christianity is. Paul's letter is not the purest expression of his—or anybody's—Christianity, but its expression when faced with a particular problem: who can be members of the Christian church and on what conditions? As he works this out, we shall see that much emerges which is very relevant for everyone who wants to know what Christianity is or who seeks to live a Christian life. Because of this the letter has continually stimulated the thought of Christians. This was especially true at the time of the Reformation when Luther, Calvin, and the other leaders of Protestantism drew much of their inspiration from it. If at that time the interpretation of Romans was strongly contested between Roman Catholics and Protestants, it is true that today they are drawing much closer to a common understanding of it.

Paul wrote this letter when he was in Corinth, or shortly after he had left it on his way to Jerusalem with the collection (Acts 20:1–3). He had come to Corinth where there had been some dispute about his authority; this had been settled, and he remained for some months until the money had arrived from other churches to be taken to Jerusalem. It is impossible to be certain of the absolute date because Paul's letter contains no reference to the major events in the history of the Roman Empire which can be precisely dated: it must however have been written in the period A.D. 55–9. Paul was now fairly sure of his future plans and since he hoped the Roman Church would play a considerable part in them, he writes to the Christians there introducing himself to them.

✼   ✼   ✼   ✼   ✼   ✼   ✼   ✼   ✼   ✼   ✼   ✼   ✼

The Gospel according to Paul

PAUL INTRODUCES HIMSELF

FROM PAUL, servant of Christ Jesus, apostle by God's **1** call, set apart for the service of the Gospel.

This gospel God announced beforehand in sacred scrip- **2** tures through his prophets. It is about his Son: on the **3** human level he was born of David's stock, but on the level **4** of the spirit—the Holy Spirit—he was declared Son of God by a mighty act in that he rose from the dead: it is about Jesus Christ our Lord. Through him I received the **5** privilege of a commission in his name to lead to faith and obedience men in all nations, yourselves among them, you **6** who have heard the call and belong to Jesus Christ.

I send greetings to all of you in Rome whom God loves **7** and has called to be his dedicated people. Grace and peace to you from God our Father and the Lord Jesus Christ.

* In Paul's day, letters began with the sender's name, followed by that of the person or persons to whom it was sent and a greeting: *A* to *B*, Greetings. Each part of this formula might be expanded if the writer wished. In our passage, verse 1 corresponds to *A* and verse 7 to *B* and the greeting. Verses 2–6 are an expansion of *A*. Since Paul was unknown in person to most of the Christians in Rome he introduces himself, carefully explaining in verses 1 and 5 his authority and in 2–4 showing that the Gospel he preaches is the same as the Gospel they already know.

1. *Servant*, or 'slave', may be used of every Christian, because he serves Jesus; *apostle* is reserved for a few. The latter word is used both in a narrow sense of the twelve disciples of Jesus and in a wider sense of all who are 'sent' (this is the literal meaning of the word) by Jesus to proclaim the Gospel. Paul uses it here in

9

the narrower sense; he had not been a disciple of the earthly Jesus but claims an equality with the original twelve disciples because he has been *set apart for the service of the Gospel*. Elsewhere he argues that he is 'an apostle, not by human appointment or human commission, but by commission from Jesus Christ and from God the Father' (Gal. 1:1); he is such in order that he 'might proclaim' Christ 'among the Gentiles' (Gal. 1:15–16). His commission was recognized by the original apostles who acknowledged that he 'had been entrusted with the Gospel for Gentiles as surely as Peter had been entrusted with the Gospel for Jews' (Gal. 2:7). Thus Paul's authority to address the Roman Christians is that of an *apostle* like one of the twelve chosen by Jesus, and his special sphere of responsibility is the Gentiles, i.e. non-Jews. Paul is throughout conscious of God's call to this (cf. verse 5), and therein he resembles many of the prophets of the Old Testament, e.g. Isaiah, Jeremiah; they too thought of themselves as the 'servants' of God.

2. *sacred scriptures*: if Paul thinks and feels like a prophet of the Old Testament it is not surprising that he sees his *gospel* (literally, 'good news') as a continuance and fulfilment of the message of the Old Testament. The relationship of the new thing that has happened in Jesus to the older story of the Old Testament is one of the themes of the letter. Since some of his readers may have heard that Paul is a revolutionary who thinks all the teaching of the Old Testament unimportant, he seeks now to disarm them, claiming to base his teaching on the Old Testament itself.

3–4. From the very first, Christians would have been forced to say what the centre of their belief was, both as an acknowledgement of their own acceptance of it when they were being baptized and in order to be able to explain it to others. Thus brief creeds or confessions grew up. Paul now takes up one of these which would have been known to his correspondents. There are two elements in this brief statement: the first connects Jesus to the Royal House of *David*, of which the Jews expected their Messiah to be a descendant; the second proclaims him as God's *Son*, because of his resurrection. The second of these is not the way Paul always puts it, but he is content to express himself by means of a statement with which his readers are familiar. Paul regarded Jesus as God's Son even in the time before he was born of Mary; cf. 'God sent his own Son, born of a woman' (Gal. 4:4). It is probable that the Greek word translated *declared* in verse 4 should be rendered 'designated' or 'chosen'; these are the meanings it has in Acts 10:42 and 17:31 respectively. The primitive church took time to express its understanding of Jesus, and it would seem at first to have connected his sonship to his resurrection as in the brief creed quoted here; we find such a view in the early sermons preached by Peter in Acts. Nearer to this view is the alternative translation of the footnote in the N.E.B.: 'declared Son of God with full powers from the time when he rose from the dead'. Fairly soon the church came to the view that Jesus existed as God's Son before his birth, which is the view Paul usually maintains. Discussion continued and was only finally formalized for the early church by the councils of the bishops of the church meeting in the fourth and fifth centuries. The Nicene Creed is one of these formulations; it will be found in the Book of Common Prayer and in many hymn books. Other early brief statements of the belief of the primitive church probably underlie 4:24-5; 10:8-10. Our present statement sets out Jesus as belonging to two spheres of existence: he is *human* as a descendant of *David*, divine as the *Son of God*.

5. *faith and obedience* go inextricably together. Only in obedience is there faith, for faith is not emotional feeling or intellectual acceptance but active response to a person, God; it is trust. Faith in a person creates the relationship in which it is easy to accept his guidance, and so to obey him. It is difficult to obey someone you do not trust. For *faith* see also p. 17.

6-7. The 'commission' (verse 5) which God gave to Paul includes all the Christians of Rome. Like Paul, they have *heard the call*. God calls men, not only the few to be apostles, but all to be followers of Jesus, for all followers serve him. So Jesus was said

11

to have 'called' his first disciples, Peter, Andrew, James, John (Mark 1:16–20). Those whom God calls are his *dedicated people*. This does not mean that they have dedicated themselves and live perfect lives, but that God in his mercy has chosen them to be his people as the Jews had been. Like Paul they are 'set apart for the service of the Gospel' (verse 1), though not as apostles.

Grace and peace in combination as a term of greeting seems to have originated in the Christian church; *peace* by itself was the normal Jewish greeting and a word like *grace* was used by Greeks. God is showing them his favour (*grace*), or else they would not be Christians, and he is at *peace* with them; *peace* refers not to an inward peace of heart, so that they feel at ease, but to God's relation to them (cf. 5:1, 10). ✳

PAUL'S PRAYERS FOR THE CHURCH AT ROME

8 Let me begin by thanking my God, through Jesus Christ, for you all, because all over the world they are telling the
9 story of your faith. God is my witness, the God to whom I offer the humble service of my spirit by preaching the gospel of his Son: God knows how continually I make
10 mention of you in my prayers, and am always asking that by his will I may, somehow or other, succeed at long last in
11 coming to visit you. For I long to see you; I want to bring
12 you some spiritual gift to make you strong; or rather, I want to be among you to receive encouragement myself through the influence of your faith on me as of mine on you.

✳ As was customary in ancient letters, Paul continues with a thanksgiving—the only letter in which he omits this is Galatians—and a prayer for his correspondents. He desires to visit them that they may grow mutually in their faith.

8. Rome was the capital of the world and what happened

there was both known in other places and an example to them. Paul says much the same kind of thing to the church at Thessalonica (1 Thess. 1:7) and therefore is not making a flattering appeal to the sense of importance of his readers simply because they live in the capital. *Faith* here does not mean the content of what they believe or their personal trust in God but rather their faithfulness; because they trust God they obey him.

9. Since they cannot know for certain that Paul is praying for them he solemnly calls *God* to *witness*. Paul's *service* to God includes *preaching* and *prayer*; the latter a service offered when he is absent from his readers. He offers this *service* of his *spirit*, i.e. of his whole being. When Paul speaks here of his own *spirit* he is not thinking of something spiritual or mystical, remote from ordinary living, but of putting all of himself into his *preaching*.

11. Paul does not say with what *spiritual gift* he will help the church; the extensive variety of such gifts is indicated in 12:6–8; cf. 1 Cor. 12:4–11. Only the actual situation will produce the relevant gift with which, as an apostle, Paul will minister to them.

12. But the ministry in spiritual gifts is mutual. Because Paul and his readers belong to the one church which is the Body of Christ (12:3–8), when they give they also receive. In saying that he will *receive encouragement* from them, Paul is not just being tactful but is stating a profound fact of Christian experience. Since his ultimate desire is to go beyond Rome to Spain (15:23; see p. 6) he would like to be able to look on Rome not just as a stage on his journey but as a base from which he can draw spiritual refreshment. But even this might suggest that he only wishes to make use of the Roman church and so in verse 13 he makes it clear that he wishes to see them for their own sake.   ✳

PAUL'S APOSTOLIC DUTY

But I should like you to know, my brothers, that I have 13
often planned to come, though so far without success, in the
hope of achieving something among you, as I have in

14 other parts of the world. I am under obligation to Greek and
15 non-Greek, to learned and simple; hence my eagerness to declare the Gospel to you in Rome as well as to others.

✻ Paul's mission was to all the Gentiles (see notes on 1:1); since Rome was the world's capital and a Gentile city his apostolic commission therefore includes it; he is eager to come and has tried to make arrangements to do so, but for reasons he does not disclose has so far been prevented.

13. *brothers*: a term used in the church from the beginning for fellow believers. It was used also in various Jewish and Greek religious communities, but its Christian usage probably goes back to Jesus himself, who says that the person who 'does the will of God is my brother, my sister, my mother' (Mark 3:35), and to the church's own deep feeling of itself as the family of God (cf. 12:10, 13).

14. *Greek and non-Greek*: not a definition in terms of race, language or nation; it is roughly equivalent to 'cultured and un-cultured' and is similar to the second contrast, *learned and simple*. This is a 'Greek' way of classifying mankind, for the Greeks regarded most other nations as 'barbarians' and 'unlearned'. Many nations have liked to think of themselves in the same way. The Jews also contrasted themselves with the rest of mankind, the Gentiles (cf. 1:16; 3:29). Rome was a centre of Greek culture and many of Paul's readers would have regarded themselves as 'Greeks' in the sense defined. ✻

THE TEXT OF THE EPISTLE

16   For I am not ashamed of the Gospel. It is the saving power of God for everyone who has faith—the Jew first,
17 but the Greek also—because here is revealed God's way of righting wrong, a way that starts from faith and ends in faith; as Scripture says, 'he shall gain life who is justified through faith'.

✻ Through the personal statement at the beginning of verse 16 Paul moves to the discussion which forms the main part of the letter and in which he expounds the message of the Gospel with its equal relevance for Jew and non-Jew. Essentially it is God's goodness in righting wrong, i.e. in saving man; and it thereby calls forth man's faith so that he lives.

16. The *Gospel* offends many people because it does not appear to give a large enough place either to art, literature, science and culture generally or to the goodness man attains apart from it. Paul is aware of this, but because he also knows its *saving power* he is *not ashamed* of it even in Rome, the world's capital. The Gospel saves men from the 'divine retribution' (1:18; 5:9–10) which should fall on them for their sins. This salvation is for all men, *Jew* and *Greek*, i.e. Jew and non-Jew, because, so far as man is concerned, it is based not on race or colour but on *faith*. The Jew then has no advantage over the non-Jew. However the relationship of Jew and non-Jew is not quite so simple as this would suggest. God's activity began with the Jews (*the Jew first*) and was disclosed in his choice of them as his People, but now it is *revealed* as directed towards all men (*the Greek also*). To the present and future relationship of Jew and Gentile Paul will return in chapters 9–11.

17. God's 'saving Power' is his *way of righting wrong*. The Greek words which are here translated *righting wrong* and *justified* come from the same Greek root *dikaioun*. God's 'justice' (3:21, 25, 26) and 'righteousness' (4:3, 5, etc.) are also from it. With these phrases we encounter the doctrine of 'justification by faith'. The terms used by Paul come from legal usage; but Hebrew justice was different from Greek and modern Western justice, and the correct background for understanding the words is the Old Testament. In it we meet a God who has chosen a people and entered into a covenant with them; he will expect obedience from them, but he will also regard them as his people and will act to help them. If he is their judge, then it is as one who seeks to help those who have been oppressed, who actively seeks to set right what is wrong.

The ideal of the true judge is set out in Ps. 82:3–4, 'Judge the poor and fatherless: Do justice to the afflicted and destitute. Rescue the poor and needy: Deliver them out of the hand of the wicked.' Thus when God is just (i.e. acting as a good judge) he will set out to save his people. This is brought out most clearly in Isa. 40–55 (often termed 'Second-Isaiah'; it is a part of the book of Isaiah which comes from the sixth century B.C. when many of the Jews had been exiled to Babylon) and in some of the Psalms, where righteousness and salvation are set in parallel as interchangeable terms; e.g. Isa. 51:5–6, 'My righteousness is near, my salvation is gone forth ... but my salvation shall be for ever, and my righteousness shall not be abolished'; Ps. 71:15, 'My mouth shall tell of thy righteousness, And of thy salvation all the day' (cf. Isa. 46:13; 61:10). There are also times when 'righteousness' practically comes to mean 'victory', e.g. Isa. 41:10, 'I will uphold thee with the right hand of my righteousness', where the R.S.V. translates 'with my victorious right hand'. Of particular interest to us is Ps. 98:2, 'The Lord hath made known his salvation: his righteousness hath he openly shewed in the sight of the nations', because we find here, as in Rom. 1:16–17, salvation and righteousness shown (revealed) to all the nations (Jew and Greek). Although these passages in the Old Testament were written long before Paul, the conception they embodied was kept alive, and we find it reappearing in some of the Dead Sea Scrolls.

'God's righteousness', as referred to by Second-Isaiah and the Psalmists, is the phrase rendered *God's way of righting wrong* in our passage; thus to say 'God is righteous' is almost equivalent to saying 'God saves'. So when Paul in 3:26 speaks of God as 'just' (which is the same word as 'righteous') he does not mean that God judges men by some abstract principle of justice in accordance with their good and evil deeds, but that God is active to right wrong. In the Old Testament God was most often pictured as righting the wrongs suffered by his People and as punishing the other nations. For Paul all men are the object of God's saving activity, and their justification (being set right) takes place through their *faith*.

faith: note how often in verses 16–17 this word appears. It is fundamental for Paul. It is easier to say what it is not than what it is. It is not a system of belief ('the Christian faith') nor an emotional feeling; it is not 'faithfulness' to a system or organization. It is called out by the way in which God has given his Son to save men; it is the attitude to which man is awakened when he sees that God has done this for him and when he, man, does not ignore it but willingly associates himself with it. It is openness towards God and what he will do. It is negative in the sense that there is no striving after some reward or recognition from God; it is positive in the sense that man leaves to God what he cannot do for himself. It is thus a possibility for both Jew and Greek. Paul refers many times to it in the letter, and each time we learn a little more of what it is.

Finally, in verse 17 Paul quotes from Hab. 2:4. His citation follows neither the Hebrew nor its Greek translation, the Septuagint (see notes on 2:23–4). He may have been quoting from memory or using a version which we do not possess to-day, or he may have altered the passage to bring out what he held to be its latent meaning. (For the way Paul uses the Old Testament see pp. 52–3.) He thus calls in the Old Testament to show that his doctrine is not new but ancient (1:2), and throughout the letter he quotes regularly from the Old Testament. Those who are set right by God are termed *justified*. As we read on in the letter we shall see that this neither means that they are falsely written up as 'righteous' when they are not, nor that God suddenly transforms them into perfect beings; but it does mean that their sins are forgiven, that they are acquitted of their faults by God. Here Paul is content to say very briefly that when God 'rights wrong' for men they *gain life*; later in the epistle Paul will work out the nature of this *life*; like the righteousness of a justified man, it is real and not fictitious.

Paul has now given us his text, and his exposition is to follow.

In 1:18 — 3:20 he will show us that all men are in need of being set right; in 3:21 — 4:25 he will tell us more about how God does 'right wrong'; in 5:1 — 8:39 he will speak of the 'life' man 'gains' when he is set right; in 9:1 — 11:36 he will show how Jew and Gentile are related in this to one another; and finally in 12:1 — 15:13 he will speak of the demands of the new life for day-by-day righteousness. *

THE ANGER OF GOD REVEALED AGAINST (*a*) ALL MEN

18 For we see divine retribution revealed from heaven and falling upon all the godless wickedness of men. In their
19 wickedness they are stifling the truth. For all that may be known of God by men lies plain before their eyes; indeed
20 God himself has disclosed it to them. His invisible attributes, that is to say his everlasting power and deity, have been visible, ever since the world began, to the eye of reason, in the things he has made. There is therefore no pos-
21 sible defence for their conduct; knowing God, they have refused to honour him as God, or to render him thanks. Hence all their thinking has ended in futility, and their mis-
22 guided minds are plunged in darkness. They boast of their
23 wisdom, but they have made fools of themselves, exchanging the splendour of immortal God for an image shaped like mortal man, even for images like birds, beasts, and creeping things.

24   For this reason God has given them up to the vileness of their own desires, and the consequent degradation of their
25 bodies, because they have bartered away the true God for a false one, and have offered reverence and worship to created things instead of to the Creator, who is blessed for ever; amen.

26   In consequence, I say, God has given them up to shame-

ful passions. Their women have exchanged natural inter-
course for unnatural, and their men in turn, giving up 27
natural relations with women, burn with lust for one another; males behave indecently with males, and are paid in
their own persons the fitting wage of such perversion.

Thus, because they have not seen fit to acknowledge 28
God, he has given them up to their own depraved reason.
This leads them to break all rules of conduct. They are 29
filled with every kind of injustice, mischief, rapacity, and
malice; they are one mass of envy, murder, rivalry, treach-
ery, and malevolence; whisperers and scandal-mongers, 30
hateful to God, insolent, arrogant, and boastful; they in-
vent new kinds of mischief, they show no loyalty to parents,
no conscience, no fidelity to their plighted word; they are 31
without natural affection and without pity. They know 32
well enough the just decree of God, that those who behave
like this deserve to die, and yet they do it; not only so, they
actually applaud such practices.

* If God is to 'right wrong' (1: 17) it must be first clearly seen
that there is wrong to be righted. So Paul now goes on to show
that this is so in respect of all men (1: 18–32) and then in particular that it is true of the Jews (2: 1 — 3: 8). Men need to be set
right because, although God had made himself known to them,
they rejected that knowledge; God for his part reacted against
their rejection by punishing them with sins. The knowledge
God has given them of himself leaves them without excuse and
their sins make them worthy of death. In this way God's anger
is revealed against their wickedness.

18. *divine retribution*, or more simply, 'God's anger': this
does not mean that God is subject to outbursts of passion or
dominated by a slow sulky desire to get even with those who
offend him. Most Jews of Paul's day expected that God's anger

would only be seen on the day of judgement, when men would be punished for their sins (cf. 2: 5, 8, 16). Paul says that even now *we see* God's anger *revealed*, and the remainder of 18–32 shows how this is true. There is a strong parallel here with verse 17; to bring it out we might translate this part of verse 18 as 'Here is revealed God's way of punishing wrong'. 'God's way of right-ing wrong' is already revealed, as we have seen, in the life, death and resurrection of Jesus Christ: his manner of punishing wrong is now seen in the very sins into which men fall. But while verses 17 and 18 are very similar at this point, this does not mean that God is pulled two ways at once, to right wrong and to punish it. His way of righting wrong is mentioned first and dominates the whole letter, because this is God's main purpose. Before, however, he could right wrong, men had to know their wrong: thus, before he revealed himself through Jesus as one who rights wrong, God was already seen as the one who punishes wrong, his *retribution . . . falling upon all the godless wickedness of men*. If men do not know their wrong they cannot have faith that God will save them, and they will still have to reckon with him as the one who punishes wrong.

19–21. The 'wickedness' of men lies in their not *knowing God* who has *disclosed to them* what may be known of himself. In what way has God *disclosed* knowledge of himself? *His invisible attributes, that is to say his everlasting power and deity*, are *visible*. His *attributes* are his qualities or characteristics; the two which Paul selects here are his *power* and his *deity*, the latter being that which would call out reverence and worship on man's part. These are *visible* to the *eye* of the mind. Since it is said that they *have been visible, ever since the world began*, we should think of God being known, first, in the act of creation (*the things he has made*), the greatness of the universe disclosing his *power* and majesty; and, secondly, in his direction of all that happens in the world. For his anger is revealed, i.e. is to be seen, in the affairs of men, and men 'know well enough the just decree of God, that those who behave like this [i.e. sin] deserve to die' (verse 32). Thus men may see God in what happens to them in their own lives and in the affairs of the nations. This is not just *knowing* about how God acts; Paul speaks of men as *knowing God*, i.e. in the way we know a person whom we meet daily, rather than one of whom we read in a book. Paul assumes that all of us know about the existence of God from what we see and so does not just say that we can deduce his existence therefrom; rather we ought to learn that he is a God of *power* and majesty. We should further note that Paul does not say that we can deduce from the type of world in which we live that God 'rights wrong'—this can only be known through Jesus; nor does Paul say that men have to search for God; God has revealed himself to them.

The man who accepts God's disclosure will *honour him as God* and *render him thanks*. But men, while this disclosure is *plain before their eyes*, have not accepted it; this failure is seen in their lack of obedience to God; thus they *have no possible defence for their conduct*. Furthermore, their rejection of God's self-disclosure has led to the corruption of their own ability to reason correctly: *their thinking* ends *in futility*, leading to no useful or good conclusion, and the *mind*, without the light that the knowledge of God gives, loses itself in *darkness*, and is unable to guide human conduct correctly.

22–3. Being in darkness, men do not understand that they have gone astray, but think that their thought and conduct are good, and so they *boast of their wisdom*. In fact they are *fools*; having failed to see the power and majesty of God they have an utterly wrong idea of him, and imagine that his nature is like that of the things they know and see from day to day, that he is like *mortal man* or some animal, bird or fish. Paul does not say that men after rejecting God turned away from religion but that they fell into wrong ways of serving God, false religions; there were few people in Paul's day who did not believe in some god or offer some kind of worship. Many people do not consciously worship God but still say they believe in him; they run the same danger of *exchanging the splendour of immortal God* for an idea of God which they have worked out for themselves or picked up from others; if the God they have is not the God we learn about in Jesus then it will be a God thought out by mortal man and therefore like *mortal man*.

24–31. Their failure to respond to the knowledge of God leads first to corruption of their thought (verses 21–2), then to idolatrous worship (verse 23). God's 'retribution' (verse 18) is now seen to work itself out in three stages: three times Paul says *God has given them up to* ... (24, 26, 28). This does not just mean that God has made the world in such a way that sin inevitably draws its own punishment, like some natural process as when drought kills vegetation. God, rather, takes active steps to punish those who reject him; and this very punishment means that men sin in ever greater degree. It is not that sin leads men to reject God but that the rejection of God is punished by sin. (*a*) When men offer *reverence and worship to created things* they themselves, who are *created things*, are led astray into the *degradation of their bodies* (verses 24–5). (*b*) This leads on from the excessive *desire* for what is *natural* to the *lust* for unnatural sexual relations, the perversion of the natural (verses 26–7). (*c*) The ultimate stage is the breaking of *all rules of conduct*, and here God's anger works out in personal relationships that have gone all wrong (verses 28–31). In these three stages Paul depicts the heathen society of his day; not all who lived in it were as bad as he suggests here, as we shall see in 2: 14–15, 25–9; a good life is thus possible apart from the Jewish law. He can also describe Christian conduct in terms drawn from the Greek ideal of behaviour: 'And now, my friends, all that is true, all that is noble, all that is just and pure, all that is lovable and gracious, whatever is excellent and admirable—fill all your thoughts with these things' (Phil. 4: 8). We should not therefore conclude that every non-Christian civilization closely resembles what Paul describes here, nor that the Greek civilization of his day was unrelieved by any idea of goodness.

25. *the Creator, who is blessed for ever*: in Jewish fashion Paul adds a doxology (a formula ascribing glory to God): all men should be praising God in the same way as he does, instead of choosing the *created* for the *Creator*.

26–7. Homosexuality not only often went uncondemned in the ancient world but was sometimes even glorified as a stage of love higher than that between man and woman.

32. Men *know well enough* how God will act, for they know at the very least how God has shown his retribution, and so they are guilty. Their wrong is the greater because they not only sin but do so with an easy conscience, *applauding* sin and holding it to be good. ✳

2: I — 3: 8 THE ANGER OF GOD REVEALED
AGAINST (*b*) THE JEWS

2: I–IO THEY MUST MEET GOD'S JUDGEMENT

You therefore have no defence—you who sit in judge- **2** ment, whoever you may be—for in judging your fellow- man you condemn yourself, since you, the judge, are equally guilty. It is admitted that God's judgement is 2 rightly passed upon all who commit such crimes as these; and do you imagine—you who pass judgement on the 3 guilty while committing the same crimes yourself—do you imagine that you, any more than they, will escape the judgement of God? Or do you think lightly of his wealth 4 of kindness, of tolerance, and of patience, without recog- nizing that God's kindness is meant to lead you to a change of heart? In the rigid obstinacy of your heart you are laying 5 up for yourself a store of retribution for the day of retribu- tion, when God's just judgement will be revealed, and he 6 will pay every man for what he has done. To those who 7 pursue glory, honour, and immortality by steady persis- tence in well-doing, he will give eternal life; but for those 8 who are governed by selfish ambition, who refuse obedi- ence to the truth and take the wrong for their guide, there will be the fury of retribution. There will be grinding 9

misery for every human being who is an evil-doer, for the
10 Jew first and for the Greek also; and for every well-doer
there will be glory, honour, and peace, for the Jew first and
also for the Greek.

∗ Paul now turns to those, especially Jews, who like himself
would criticize the failings of pagan society and claim to be
superior to it, and so expect to escape God's anger. He argues
that they are not entitled to expect this but must face that anger.

1–2. In sharp contrast with 1: 32, where Paul speaks of those
who 'applaud' the sins of pagan society, we now meet those
who condemn them. It is not clear whether Paul has in mind
Jews alone or possibly also those within pagan society who were
critical of it. Certainly by the time he reaches 2: 17 Paul is dealing with Jews only, but what he says in 2: 1–10 applies to anyone who takes up the position of a critic of the sins of society.
Paul rounds sharply on such a person, who will of course have
agreed with what he wrote in 1: 18–32. Like the sinning pagan
they *have no defence* (cf. 1: 20) and Paul will show that they *are
equally guilty*. So they will equally merit God's 'retribution'
(verses 5, 8) 'on the day when God judges the secrets of human
hearts' (verse 16).

3. *committing the same crimes*: Paul does not mean that they
commit the actual sins of 1: 29–31, though in 2: 21–3 he accuses
the Jews of similar offences. He may be thinking either that,
since they set themselves up as judges, they are usurping the
function of God and so are making God in their own image
(1: 23), or he may have in mind a deeper conception of sin. In
Matt. 5: 21–48 Jesus shows that sin cannot be limited to outward actions or words but involves also the inner motive,
though it may never be realized in actual behaviour; this
deepening of thought as to what is sin is summarized in words
from 1 John 3: 15, 'everyone who hates his brother is a
murderer'. (See also note on 2: 21–2.)

4–5. The Jews sometimes thought of the period before the
day of *judgement* as intended by God in his *tolerance* and *patience*

to give the Gentiles an opportunity to repent and escape his anger; Paul now turns this thought against themselves. We may note that throughout this section (2: 1 — 3: 8) Paul no longer thinks of God's anger as revealed now but rather as something which will be seen fully in a day of final judgement (cf. verses 5, 8, 16).

6. This verse is really a quotation from Ps. 62: 12, where the Psalmist expresses his confidence that God will deliver him from his enemies because *what he has done* is good. This, which would express the general view of the Jews of Paul's day and of most people in every age in respect of themselves, is used by Paul against them; since what they have done is not good, they will have to meet God's anger in the day of retribution. The verse sums up what has been said in verses 1–5 and prepares us for the further step of verses 7–10 in which it is made clear in what way *God will pay every man for what he has done*.

The use of this quotation might suggest that men are accepted by God on the basis of *what* they have *done*, i.e. on the basis of their behaviour. This would appear to conflict with what Paul has already said about God righting wrong: it is he who saves men—not what they themselves do. We shall see in 3: 20, 28 that Paul refutes the idea that man can deliver himself from God's judgement by what he does. Rather God 'justifies any man who puts his faith in Jesus' (3: 26). In our present passage Paul has in mind the man who does not know God's way of righting wrong (1: 17); he is either the Jew who has been given God's Law or the good pagan who has accepted God's disclosure of himself (1: 19 f.) and has the law written on his heart (2: 14 f.); such men will be judged by God on their deeds. But, once God's way of righting wrong was revealed in Jesus, a new situation was created and in respect of that Paul will go on to draw the conclusion that in actual fact no man can hope to receive any reward from God for *what he has done* (3: 19 f., 23).

9–10. Notice that Paul mentions the Jew *first* in speaking of both the *evil-doer* and the *well-doer*. God looks first at the people whom the Old Testament tells us he chose to be his own

whenever he wishes either to right wrong or to punish it. Amos
3: 1–2 expresses this, 'Hear this word that the Lord hath spoken
against you, O children of Israel... You only have I known of
all the families of the earth: therefore I will visit upon you all
your iniquities.' *

THE SAME JUDGEMENT FOR JEW AND GENTILE

11,12 For God has no favourites: those who have sinned outside
the pale of the Law of Moses will perish outside its pale, and
all who have sinned under that law will be judged by the
13 law. It is not by hearing the law, but by doing it, that men
14 will be justified before God. When Gentiles who do not
possess the law carry out its precepts by the light of nature,
then, although they have no law, they are their own law,
15 for they display the effect of the law inscribed on their
hearts. Their conscience is called as witness, and their own
thoughts argue the case on either side, against them or even
16 for them, on the day when God judges the secrets of human
hearts through Christ Jesus. So my gospel declares.

* Paul continues to speak of what happens to men apart from
the revelation of God's saving power in Jesus. There is no
ultimate difference between Jew and Gentile; both know
God's will and both will be judged in respect of how they
keep it.

Before we consider these verses it is necessary to say a little
about a word which we find Paul continually using in this
letter: the *law*. The conception of 'the Law' was central to the
Jewish religion; the term itself was used in different ways.
It could mean the set of laws which God gave to the Jews at
the time of the Exodus: at its simplest this consisted of the
Ten Commandments (Exod. 20: 1–20; Deut. 5). The word
was more usually taken to include all the laws of the first
five books of the Bible (Genesis–Deuteronomy, often termed

'the Pentateuch', literally 'the five books') which the Jews believed to have been written by Moses (hence it comes to be called *the Law of Moses*). The law was also often taken to include all the laws and interpretations of laws which had been developed by the Jews after the Pentateuch had finally been put together (this is believed to have been about the fourth or fifth century B.C.). Whichever meaning it has, the law includes both regulations which refer to moral conduct, e.g. 'Thou shalt not kill' (the sixth commandment), and those which deal with matters of ritual, e.g. the laws about the kinds of food which a Jew should or should not eat.

In our letter Paul is largely concerned with the laws relating to moral behaviour, and he uses 'law' in the sense of a systematic code of ethics. Because this code was largely drawn from the Pentateuch, he can sometimes refer to the latter as 'the Law'; this indeed was the most important part of the Old Testament for the Jew. But the very fact that Paul can use the term to suggest something wider than a set of laws (e.g. in 3 : 19, as meaning the whole Old Testament) shows that it has further meanings. It can mean the Jewish religion as a whole—the way of life in which obedience to God is primary. God calls for this obedience, however, only because of what he has done for Israel. Thus the Ten Commandments are prefaced with: 'I am the Lord thy God, which brought thee out of the land of Egypt, out of the house of bondage' (Exod. 20: 2). The law was thus given by God only because he wished to save Israel, and so the Psalmist can say: 'Oh how love I thy law! It is my meditation all the day' (Ps. 119: 97). When many of the Jews of Paul's day failed to realize this and took the law to mean only obedience to a fixed set of laws they perverted their religion. It is equally perverted when it is believed that God can be obeyed so well that he will regard as a favourite the person who is obedient and will therefore accept him as 'justified' (see note on 1: 16–17). Paul shows in 2: 1 — 3: 20 that in actual fact no man obeys God well enough to please him.

It is this wider conception of the law, as a way of life in which obedience is primary, which ensures that Paul's letter is always relevant to men who wish to be religious. Whenever men think that religion is living up to a fixed standard of behaviour or fulfilling some fixed ideal of conduct, whether these are regarded as coming from God or not, then they must face the criticisms which Paul makes of religion as obedience to law.

We have only indicated the major ways in which Paul uses *law* and we shall draw attention to others as we encounter them.

11–12. The Jew would have considered himself God's *favourite* because he had been given *the Law of Moses*. But this is no real advantage to the Jew for (*a*) it is doing the law, not knowing it, that counts (verse 13), and (*b*) the Gentiles are not completely ignorant of what God wants from them (verses 14–15).

13. Throughout 2: 1–16 there is continued emphasis on actual deeds; neither moral indignation at those who sin nor a full knowledge of what is in the law is a substitute for *doing* right.

14–15. The *Gentiles* (i.e. everyone other than the Jews), to whom God gave no specific set of laws to obey like the Ten Commandments, are not left without guidance as to what God wishes them to do. Indeed even the Jew would have had to admit that Abraham, Isaac, Jacob, who lived before God gave the Law to Moses, knew and often did what God wanted. Paul says nothing about how detailed a knowledge the Gentile might have of God's will, but he argues that within the man who does not have the law *inscribed* on stone (the Ten Commandments were believed to have been written by God on two stone slabs—Deut. 5: 22) there is something which can direct him to do what is good. This is man's possession by his very *nature* and in this sense man is his own guide or *law*. He may have no outside standard of conduct but he has one *inscribed* on his *heart*. As an observable fact Gentiles *display the effect of the law* which is written within them because at times they do what is right. They are pictured as conducting a discussion within themselves as to their actions, *arguing the case on either side*. When a man goes to do wrong his *conscience* speaks against him. A man can thus abstract himself from himself to look at himself from outside and consider whether his actions are right or wrong. Paul assumes that man can do this because this is the way God has made him; the Gentiles of course may not realize that God has done this in order to help them to do right. Paul does not say that all Gentiles pay heed to their consciences, nor does he say that any particular Gentile does so consistently. He is not trying to argue that Gentiles are good, but that, because they know something of God's will, they and the Jews come under the same judgement.

16. This verse should not be so closely linked to what precedes as to suggest that man's conscience only comes into action on *the day* of judgement—when it would be too late. On that day the *secret* discussions of men's hearts and consciences will be brought to light and men's actions will be judged in relation to them. *

THE JEW CAN CLAIM NO SPECIAL PRIVILEGE AGAINST
THE ANGER OF GOD

But as for you—you may bear the name of Jew; you rely 17 upon the law and are proud of your God; you know his 18 will; you are aware of moral distinctions because you receive instruction from the law; you are confident that you 19 are the one to guide the blind, to enlighten the benighted, to train the stupid, and to teach the immature, because in 20 the law you see the very shape of knowledge and truth. You, then, who teach your fellow-man, do you fail to 21 teach yourself? You proclaim, 'Do not steal'; but are you yourself a thief? You say, 'Do not commit adultery'; but 22 are you an adulterer? You abominate false gods; but do you rob their shrines? While you take pride in the law, you 23

24 dishonour God by breaking it. For, as Scripture says, 'Because of you the name of God is dishonoured among the
Gentiles.'

25   Circumcision has value, provided you keep the law; but
if you break the law, then your circumcision is as if it had
26 never been. Equally, if an uncircumcised man keeps the
27 precepts of the law, will he not count as circumcised? He
may be uncircumcised in his natural state, but by fulfilling
the law he will pass judgement on you who break it, for all
28 your written code and your circumcision. The true Jew is
not he who is such in externals, neither is the true circum-
29 cision the external mark in the flesh. The true Jew is he who
is such inwardly, and the true circumcision is of the heart,
directed not by written precepts but by the Spirit; such a
man receives his commendation not from men but from
God.

✻ Paul now turns explicitly to the Jew. He has just argued that
all men will be judged by God on the basis of their actual deeds.
The Jew will react by arguing that he has a position of special
privilege (*a*) as the possessor of the law (verses 17–24) and (*b*) as
circumcised (verses 25–9). Paul argues that on the contrary the
privileges of the Jew offer him no protection from the judgement of God but only leave him more open to it.

17–20. The Jew through *the law* (regarded as a code of conduct given by God) had a knowledge of *moral distinctions* which
he believed it to be his duty to bring to the Gentile world,
where men were *blind* and immoral. In Paul's day there was an
active and successful Jewish mission to the Gentiles which
operated mainly through the Jewish colonies in the various
cities of the ancient world. Many Gentiles were greatly attracted to the Jewish faith because of its purer and more
spiritual worship—no multitude of gods and shrines, and,
apart from the Temple in Jerusalem, no sacrifices. Paul uses in

this passage the very terms the Jew would have used to describe this missionary activity, terms with which he himself in his pre-Christian days would have agreed. There is a certain irony in his present use of them.

21–2. The Jew breaks the very laws which he *teaches* the Gentile to keep. The instances which Paul adduces must have been of relatively infrequent occurrence, for the Jews, and especially those who would have been engaged in the mission to the Gentiles, were renowned for their moral behaviour. But also, of course, the picture which Paul draws of the Gentile world in 1: 18–32 is not a picture of the normal but of the extreme into which the Gentile world might, and at times did, fall. It may be that Paul has also in mind the way in which Jesus sharpened the meaning of the law (see note on 2: 3). Jesus said: 'You have learned that they [i.e. the Jews of old] were told, "Do not commit adultery." But what I tell you is this: If a man looks on a woman with a lustful eye, he has already committed adultery with her in his heart' (Matt. 5: 27 f.). Equally, *stealing* might be deepened into covetousness. In *do you rob their shrines* the word *their* is not in the original and *shrines* can be taken as a singular; the contrast may then be: *You abominate false gods*; but do you rob the shrine (of your own God by not giving to the upkeep of your religion, and so in fact reducing God to the level of an idol)? If it is taken as it stands in the N.E.B., it means that some Jews had been stealing from heathen temples, enriching themselves from religions in which they did not believe.

23–4. *The law* is not something in whose possession a man may *take pride*, but something which must be obeyed; anything else *dishonours* God.

Verse 24 comes from Isa. 52: 5. If an English translation of this verse is looked up it will be found to be slightly different: 'my name continually all the day is blasphemed'. We shall see that this is true of a number of Paul's quotations from the Old Testament. English Old Testaments are translated from the Hebrew, in which language the authors of the Old Testament wrote. But in Paul's day there was already a translation of the

Hebrew into Greek, the language in which Paul was writing. This translation was known as the Septuagint (often abbreviated as LXX) because it was believed to have been translated out of the Hebrew by seventy translators (septuagint = 70). It did not entirely follow the Hebrew as we know it. Paul normally uses it in his quotations, as he has done here, and so these are not always the same as the words of our English versions of the Old Testament. Sometimes he allows his knowledge of the original Hebrew to affect his quotation in Greek so that he produces a version similar to what we have in the English.

25. Paul conceives the Jew as raising another objection: 'I am *circumcised*.' Official Jewish teaching held that the circumcised Jew would be saved in the day of judgement and need not therefore worry about the retribution of God. According to the story in Gen. 17: 1–14, when God chose Abraham and his descendants to be his people he prescribed this rite for the males among them. Many ancient peoples (and some today) practised the rite of circumcision, but among the Jews it came to be regarded as the sign that they were God's people. Since God had also prescribed *the law* for his people, *circumcision* became the outward sign of one who lived by *the law*. Paul argues that this connexion between *the law* and *circumcision* cannot be severed and that therefore to *break the law* renders the Jew's *circumcision* invalid, and he becomes subject to God's judgement in the same way as the Gentile who has not been circumcised.

26–7. Paul goes much further than his statement of verse 25 in arguing that if a *man keeps . . . the law* God will *count* him as if he were circumcised. *Count* is a word that reappears at 4: 4 and implies that God will accept and save the man. The man who so *keeps . . . the law* will at God's *judgement* be a witness against the Jew who has broken it. In a very similar way Jesus said, 'At the Judgement, when this generation is on trial, the men of Nineveh [who were Gentiles] will appear against it and ensure its condemnation, for they repented at the preaching of Jonah; and what is here is greater than Jonah' (Matt. 12: 41).

28–9. *The true* member of God's chosen people (i.e. *the true Jew*) is the man who carries out God's will. Even in the time of the Old Testament it had already been realized that *external circumcision* was of no avail without the *circumcision of the heart*: 'And the Lord thy God will circumcise thine heart, and the heart of thy seed, to love the Lord thy God with all thine heart, and with all thy soul, that thou mayest live' (Deut. 30: 6). But the Old Testament had not gone so far as to argue, as Paul appears to, that *external circumcision* was of no avail at all. *Spirit* is here spelt with a capital 'S', implying that Paul is thinking not of the human spirit but of the Spirit of God (see note on 8: 3–4). *the true circumcision . . . of the heart* is not man's achievement in keeping the *written precepts* of the Law, but God's work in a man's heart by his Spirit (cf. Deut. 30: 6, quoted above). From all this the conclusion follows that circumcision does not ensure salvation, and the Jew cannot depend on his privileges to escape the judgement of God. ✻

HAS THE JEW ANY ADVANTAGE OVER THE GENTILE?

Then what advantage has the Jew? What is the value of 3 circumcision? Great, in every way. In the first place, the 2 Jews were entrusted with the oracles of God. What if some 3 of them were unfaithful? Will their faithlessness cancel the faithfulness of God? Certainly not! God must be true 4 though every man living were a liar; for we read in Scripture, 'When thou speakest thou shalt be vindicated, and win the verdict when thou art on trial.'

Another question: if our injustice serves to bring out 5 God's justice, what are we to say? Is it unjust of God (I speak of him in human terms) to bring retribution upon us? Cer- 6 tainly not! If God were unjust, how could he judge the world?

7 Again, if the truth of God brings him all the greater
honour because of my falsehood, why should I any longer
8 be condemned as a sinner? Why not indeed 'do evil that
good may come', as some libellously report me as saying?
To condemn such men as these is surely no injustice.

☆ Paul has shown that both Gentiles (1: 18–32) and Jews (2: 1–29) are sinners. Before finally making this conclusion explicit he turns aside to an imaginary Jewish objector who, because of Paul's references to circumcision, asks whether in the end being a Jew means anything at all.

1. If 'circumcision . . . of the heart' is more important than circumcision of the flesh (2: 29) and if an 'uncircumcised' Gentile is acceptable to God (2: 26), *What is the value of circumcision?* Yet there is also a real sense in which *the Jew* is 'first' (1: 16) and has *the advantage*: it lies in the fact that his people were chosen by God. Here is a problem which Paul is aware every Jew would raise, and which he probably had to answer many times in discussion with them. God commanded the Jew to circumcise himself; is this then nothing, and does God's commandment become irrelevant? If we answer that it is nothing, as 2: 25–9 might seem to suggest, then we run the danger of making the whole story of the Old Testament meaningless.

2. Paul begins his answer but he never completes his *in the first place* with other instances; 9: 4–5 indicates what he might have said were the other advantages of the Jews: they were made God's sons, they possessed the splendour of the divine presence, the covenants, the law, the temple worship, the promises, the patriarchs; and the Messiah would be a Jew: we may note he does not include circumcision among them. Circumcision is not important in itself but only as a sign of what God has *entrusted* to the Jews. Primarily they have been *entrusted with the oracles of God;* these are God's promises in the Old Testament. They do not belong to the Jews but are *entrusted* to them to use responsibly for others.

3–4. Paul has clearly shown that *some* of the Jews were *unfaithful*, but this does not mean that God will be, or has been, unfaithful and will reject them from being his people. Paul quotes from Ps. 51: 4 as found in the Septuagint. This Psalm is a confession of sin, and the Psalmist in acknowledging his sin admits that God stands in the right (*shalt be vindicated*). The *faithlessness* of the Jew serves then only to glorify God, as the Jews' own Scriptures make clear. Paul's answer here is brief; he returns to the question much more fully in chs. 9–11.

5–6. Another objection is brought forward arising out of Paul's use of Ps. 51: 4. The phrases *God's justice* and 'thou shalt be vindicated' (verse 4) go back to the same Greek word 'justified' which we have already encountered in 1: 17 (which see). If *God's justice* is seen in his winning the 'verdict' in any comparison there may be between him and man (verse 4), then is it not unfair of God to punish man since man has only helped to show up *God's justice* by his own *injustice*? Paul simply denies the allegation: if God is *judge* of the *world* he must be just.

7–8. Yet another objection which strikes more directly at the heart of what Paul preaches: if God is seen at his best when he forgives sin (the topic of Ps. 51), why should man not sin more in order to increase God's *honour*? This is a misunderstanding of what Paul preaches in that it would suggest there is no reason for man to be good. Paul returns to this objection at 6: 1 and deals with it at length; all he does at this point is to deny it by saying that for God *to condemn* those who falsely accuse him (i.e. Paul) is *no injustice*: such unwillingness to understand what Paul preaches deserves God's rebuke. ✳

CONCLUSION: ALL MEN UNDER GOD'S WRATH

What then? Are we Jews any better off? No, not at all! 9
For we have already formulated the charge that Jews and Greeks alike are all under the power of sin. This 10
has scriptural warrant:

'There is no just man, not one;

11   No one who understands, no one who seeks God.

12   All have swerved aside, all alike have become debased;
     There is no one to show kindness; no, not one.

13   Their throat is an open grave,
     They use their tongues for treachery,
     Adders' venom is on their lips,

14   And their mouth is full of bitter curses.

15   Their feet hasten to shed blood,

16   Ruin and misery lie along their paths,

17   They are strangers to the high-road of peace,

18   And reverence for God does not enter their thoughts.'

19   Now all the words of the law are addressed, as we know,
     to those who are within the pale of the law, so that no one
     may have anything to say in self-defence, but the whole

20   world may be exposed to the judgement of God. For
     (again from Scripture) 'no human being can be justified in
     the sight of God' for having kept the law: law brings only
     the consciousness of sin.

✻ Paul draws the conclusion of this stage (1: 18 — 3: 20) of his
argument: there is no exception whatsoever to the rule that all
men are sinners and therefore cannot escape the punishment of
God.

9. The question of verse 1 is repeated but answered in a
different way. Paul has *formulated the charge that Jews and Greeks
alike are all under the power of sin*. He has shown in 1: 18 — 3: 8
that this is the actual state of affairs. Now he shows (verses
10–18) that this is what the Old Testament teaches.

the power of sin: Paul means by this something more than that
'all men sin'. Sin appears not as something abstract but almost
as if it were a personal being—a strong enemy which can sub-

jugate men. As we go on we shall see how vividly Paul depicts the hostility of sin to men.

10–18. Here is a sequence of quotations from the Old Testament set out in such a way that we can see their poetic structure, like three verses of a hymn; Paul may indeed be making use of part of an early Christian hymn. Verses 10–12 are from Ps. 14: 1–3 (which is the same as Ps. 53: 1–3); verse 13 is from Ps. 5: 9 and Ps. 140: 3; verse 14 from Ps. 10: 7; verses 15–17 from Isa. 59: 7–8; verse 18 from Ps. 36: 1. They have been chosen because they set out the many sins of men and for their stress on the inclusion of everyone in the repeated *no one, not one,* and *all.*

19. It is to this very emphasis that all are alike that the Jew would have objected: he was different from the Gentile. But the emphasis comes from his own sacred Scriptures, which were primarily *addressed* to him *within the pale of the law.* In verse 2 'the oracles of God' had been described as one of his advantages; now this 'advantage' (verse 1) proves his failure and shows that he is no different from the Gentile, for the *whole world* is *exposed to the judgement of God.* We may note that Paul uses *law* in two different senses here. At its first occurrence it means the whole Old Testament (the quotations come from Psalms and Isaiah and not exclusively from the Pentateuch, the so-called Law); at its second occurrence it means the law code of Moses.

20. The quotation is from Ps. 143: 2. Paul qualifies the absolute statement of the Psalm that *no human being can be justified in the sight of God* by adding *for having kept the law,* since he wishes to go on and argue that there is a way in which man may be *justified in the sight of God* (3: 21 — 4: 25), namely, the way of faith in Christ which he has already mentioned (1: 16–17). Paul possibly uses Ps. 143: 2 because Ps. 143:1 is a call to God in his 'righteousness' to have mercy on the Psalmist; 'righteousness' represents the same word as 'justice', the keyword of 3: 21–31. The attempt to *keep the law* does not put a man in the right before God; but Paul goes straight on to show how a man can so be put in the right (3: 21–31). The *law* however is not useless,

for it *brings... the consciousness of sin*. Note that Paul does not just say that the law makes a man aware of his sins. This is so; but by using the singular *sin* and not the plural 'sins' Paul reverts to the meaning of *sin* which we saw in verse 9—a hostile power fighting against man.

Before we move on to the next great section of the letter let us briefly retrace the way we have come in 1: 18 — 3: 20. Paul is setting out to show that if men are to be justified or put in the right before God there is only one way this can be done: that in which God himself puts right what is wrong. In fact all men need to be set right by him. Some plainly pay no heed to the true God; ignoring him, they worship idols and sin in many different ways. Others, however—and Paul is thinking primarily of the Jews but his argument embraces many more—recognize God, know that he has set up standards of conduct, and seek to keep them. Equally these fail to justify themselves before God; in actual fact they never do reach the high level of God's standards or even the standards they set for themselves, and their very claim to know them makes their failure worse. Here we can see that Paul's argument, though originally addressed to men of his own day, is of much wider application, since it includes both those who ignore God's standards, such as the Gentiles, and those who know them and try to keep them, such as the Jews. The more anyone claims to know what is right, the more will he be held responsible before God when he fails. Thus, having shown that no man by what he does or thinks can put himself in the right with God, he returns (3: 21 ff.) to the great theme of the letter—'here is revealed God's way of righting wrong, a way that starts from faith and ends in faith; as Scripture says, "he shall gain life who is justified through faith"' (1: 17). *

THE RIGHTEOUSNESS OF GOD REVEALED IN THE
DEATH OF JESUS

But now, quite independently of law, God's justice has 21
been brought to light. The Law and the prophets both bear
witness to it: it is God's way of righting wrong, effective 22
through faith in Christ for all who have such faith—all,
without distinction. For all alike have sinned, and are de- 23
prived of the divine splendour, and all are justified by 24
God's free grace alone, through his act of liberation in the
person of Christ Jesus. For God designed him to be the 25
means of expiating sin by his sacrificial death, effective
through faith. God meant by this to demonstrate his justice, because in his forbearance he had overlooked the sins
of the past—to demonstrate his justice now in the present, 26
showing that he is both himself just and justifies any man
who puts his faith in Jesus.

What room then is left for human pride? It is excluded. 27
And on what principle? The keeping of the law would not
exclude it, but faith does. For our argument is that a man is 28
justified by faith quite apart from success in keeping the law.

Do you suppose God is the God of the Jews alone? Is he 29
not the God of Gentiles also? Certainly, of Gentiles also, if 30
it be true that God is one. And he will therefore justify
both the circumcised in virtue of their faith, and the uncircumcised through their faith. Does this mean that we 31
are using faith to undermine law? By no means: we are
placing law itself on a firmer footing.

* Having shown that all men have sinned and cannot therefore justify themselves before God, Paul returns to 1: 17, and
explains and expands it. He argues that in fact God has been

righting the wrong in men by the death of Jesus; he has thus done for men what they cannot do for themselves and acquits them before himself. Paul explains the relevance of Jesus' death to God's action (verses 21-6) and affirms that because God has so acted man is left with nothing in which he can pride himself (verses 27-31).

21. *But now*: there is a decisive step forward in the argument at this point, for Paul moves from the revelation of the anger of God (1: 18 — 3: 20) to the revelation of his *justice*. There is also a strong contrast in time: the revelation of God's anger preceded the revelation of his *justice* in Jesus (cf. verses 25-6), and that latter revelation has already taken place, though we would not expect it to be known until God acts as judge at the end of the world. Advanced in time from the end to *now . . . God's justice* is seen to be something other than the demands of conduct he makes through his *law*, for it *has been brought to light independently of law*. The phrase *God's justice* is identical with that which was translated 'God's way of righting wrong' in 1: 17 (cf. 3: 22). It is the key word of the discussion in 3: 21 — 4: 25; its meaning has been discussed already at 1: 16-17. *The Law* [i.e. the Pentateuch] *and the prophets* is a regular formula denoting the Old Testament; it designates the two parts of Scripture which were read in Jewish worship. The revelation of *God's justice* thus agrees with what we find in the Old Testament; Paul has already touched on this in his quotation of Hab. 2: 4 at 1: 17, and he will deal with it again throughout chapter 4. With this argument he intends to disarm the Jew who would allege that the Christian belief in Jesus is a break with what is found in the Old Testament.

22-3. *faith* is frequently mentioned throughout this section —see note on 1: 17. It is not 'because of' man's faith that God justifies him, but *through* his *faith; faith* is not an attitude on man's part which forces God to right wrong but it is an acceptance of what God does through the death of Jesus in *righting wrong.* Just as God judges all men without favouritism (2: 11) so he will also set right all who *have faith.* It makes no difference to the one who believes whether he is Jew or Gentile, black or white, male or female, for God justifies *all, without distinction*. Equally no one can either be so good as not to require to be put in the right or so evil as to be beyond being put in the right. It is probably better to connect *all, without distinction* with what follows it than with what precedes it. There is no *distinction* between men because *all alike have sinned* (cf. 10: 12); this is what Paul has been proving in 1: 18 — 3: 20. What men's sins are and how serious they appear to be does not matter— only the fact that they *have sinned* and *are deprived of the divine splendour*. The Jews believed that Adam possessed the *divine splendour* in the garden of Eden but lost it when he sinned, and that when God would make a new world at the end of time then man would regain that *divine splendour*. Paul believes that man recovers the *divine splendour* when he is *justified* (cf. notes on 5: 2 and 8: 30).

24. What does it mean to be *justified*? We have already seen (1: 17) that this means that not only is a man acquitted, or forgiven his sins, but wrong is set right so that the man is put in the right. A judge in court acquits a man of a crime he has not committed; he has never encountered the man prior to the trial and never will again after it. God, however, has made and cared for every man who may come before him as judge, and when he acquits him of sins he has committed God does not lose sight of him. On the man's part there has been faith, a willingness to accept what God has done, so that the man and God stand in a different relationship than earlier. Indeed any two people one of whom responds to the goodness and love of the other stand thereafter in a different relationship to one another.

Moreover when a man is *justified* he has received already the sentence of God the Judge, which otherwise he would not expect until the day of Judgement at the end of the world. In this sense he is already living in the new world, or New Age, which the Jews believed God would create at the last. They expected this to happen when the Messiah would appear at the end of time; for Paul (and the Christian) the Messiah had appeared in

Jesus and so he believed himself to live already in the time of the Messiah. Thus the *justified* man is a true inhabitant of the New Age even while he lives in this world; he is therefore really just or righteous. But he is also still living in the present world and is continually tempted to sin and yields. There is then a tension between his life in the new world and in the present world. He is *justified* and yet he sins; he is just and ought to be just (cf. p. 75). This tension runs right through the letter. It is related to the new relationship which man has with God (he *is* in the right with God, and in response to God's love he seeks to be righteous), and is again hinted at in the idea of man's *liberation in the person of Christ Jesus*.

The word *liberation* has a double background: (a) the deliverance of the Israelites from Egypt in the time of Moses; (b) the emancipation of men from slavery. In the time of Paul there were many slaves and sometimes they were able to earn their freedom. The man whom God justifies is liberated. He is liberated from the anger of God; as already judged by God he does not any longer fear the 'divine retribution'. Sin has already appeared as a power inimical to man (3 : 9, 20) and is mentioned again in verse 25; it is reasonable to assume that Paul conceives of man as liberated also from sin; indeed 5 : 12 — 6 : 23 is largely taken up with this idea. The inhabitant of the New Age is to be free from sin; so the *justified* man is even now. This *act of liberation* has been carried out by God himself through the *person of Christ Jesus*, and in the context of verse 25 this means primarily through his death. Paul emphasizes strongly that God has initiated man's justification through the death of Jesus, for it happens by *God's free grace alone;* it is God's gracious action to which man can contribute absolutely nothing since he is a sinner; it is therefore *free* to man. In no way does it depend on his being a member of a particular race or people or on his keeping the law or on his good behaviour.

25-6. Paul continues his explanation of the death of Jesus with a new picture. This death was not an accident, nor was it an unfortunate happening in which God's plans were frustrated;

God himself *designed* it. Yet there is no need to look on God as an angry deity who required to be appeased or propitiated by the *sacrificial death* of his Son Jesus. In the Old Testament God had set out a system of sacrifices in which animals were killed and which was *designed* to deal with sin, i.e. to *expiate* it; sin which had not been removed was a barrier which prevented God from entering into a relation of fellowship with man; it also inevitably called out 'divine retribution' (1: 18). It is not clear whether Paul has any particular part of this sacrificial system in mind or just refers to the general conception that God had prescribed means to *expiate* the sins of men and that these means entailed *sacrificial death*.

In the Old Testament system men brought the animals for sacrifice, although God was regarded as the one who ultimately provided them. There is, however, no very obvious connexion between a man's bringing a sheep for sacrifice and his sin. In fact Paul has already made it clear that there is nothing at all which a man can do that will put him in the right with God; neither sacrificing an animal nor even keeping the moral law will justify him before God. But, as in the Old Testament, God himself has provided a way to deal with the sin of man. This new way falls into line with the system there in so far as it involves a *sacrificial death;* it is not, however, something demanded from man like an animal or good behaviour, but something freely offered for man by God himself, the death of his Son Jesus. This death not only shows men that God loves them; it *expiates*, or disposes of, their sin. Paul does not enter into this as fully as we would like or explain why a *sacrificial death* was necessary to achieve this end; he assumes it and shows that it has taken place. It is not, however, a blanket expiation for sins, making every man automatically justified before God; it only becomes *effective through faith*. *Faith*, man's response to God's action, runs all through this passage.

The remainder of verses 25-6 is exceptionally difficult. The clause *in his forbearance he had overlooked the sins of the past* cannot be a general statement that God was indifferent to sin prior to

Jesus, for in 1: 18 — 3: 20 Paul argued that in that period God's anger was already revealed against the sin of men. On the other hand, the Old Testament shows that God sometimes forgave men their sins: David was pardoned his murder of Uriah the husband of Bathsheba with whom he had committed adultery (2 Sam. chs. 11, 12; see especially 12: 13); many of the Psalms imply that God forgives (e.g. Ps. 32, quoted at 4: 7–8); and the sacrificial system of the Old Testament was intended in part to deal with sin (e.g. Lev. 16). But such forgiveness might have looked like indifference to sin rather than the act of a good judge who seeks to right wrong (see on 1: 17). So when God set forth Jesus as the *means of expiating sin* he demonstrated his *justice*, in regard to sins apparently previously *overlooked*. God has carried this out *in the present;* for Paul the death of Jesus was *in the present* in comparison with the Old Testament events. Thus God shows *that he is both himself just* [i.e. a good judge who is concerned to right wrong] *and* [therefore] *justifies* [puts in the right] *any man who puts his faith in Jesus*. Remember that Paul also found faith exercised in the Old Testament period; for he uses Old Testament passages in his discussion (1: 17), and the people of the Old Testament could be justified—in fact Abraham was (4: 3).

27–8. We return now to the Jew who always thought he had a special position—in the present connexion because the sins of some of his ancestors had been forgiven by God; so he might begin to *pride* himself. But sin is forgiven in only one way— through Jesus' sacrificial death, to which the only 'effective' (verse 25) response is *faith*. In other words, *a man is justified by faith quite apart from success in keeping the law*. Verse 28 sums up verses 21–6 and gives the reason for Paul's argument in verse 27. A man's achievement in being good (*keeping the law*) would breed *pride*; faith which is reliance on God leaves to God what we cannot do for ourselves (justify ourselves) and so *excludes pride*.

The danger in a religion of law (see note on 2: 11) is that success in obedience to it leads to *pride;* this arises whether the law is a written code like the Ten Commandments or a generally accepted standard of what is good behaviour. It is this peril which leads those who follow such religions, even though they appear to have the high ideal of serving God, into a false position which in the end separates them from God.

29–31. There is only *one God*—with this the Jew would certainly have agreed, for he repeated every day, 'Hear, O Israel: the Lord our God is one Lord' (Deut. 6: 4). Since there is only one God, there can only be one way of salvation, and for both Jew and Gentile it is through *their faith*. But *does* all *this mean* that we are *using faith to undermine law*? *Law* must be understood to mean the demand for moral behaviour based on the will of God; one expression of God's will was of course the Jewish law. Paul cannot allow such a conclusion; the man who has been set right will carry out God's will which is summed up in the law of love—'the one rule, "Love your neighbour as yourself"' (13: 9). The point is dismissed briefly here, but Paul takes it up again in greater detail in chapter 6. ✻

ABRAHAM JUSTIFIED THROUGH FAITH AND NOT CIRCUMCISION

What, then, are we to say about Abraham, our ancestor in **4** the natural line? If Abraham was justified by anything he **2** had done, then he has a ground for pride. But he has no such ground before God; for what does Scripture say? **3** 'Abraham put his faith in God, and that faith was counted to him as righteousness.' Now if a man does a piece of **4** work, his wages are not 'counted' as a favour; they are paid as debt. But if without any work to his credit he simply **5** puts his faith in him who acquits the guilty, then his faith is indeed 'counted as righteousness'. In the same sense **6** David speaks of the happiness of the man whom God 'counts' as just, apart from any specific acts of justice:

45

7 'Happy are they', he says, 'whose lawless deeds are forgiven,
8 whose sins are buried away; happy is the man whose sins
9 the Lord does not count against him.' Is this happiness
confined to the circumcised, or is it for the uncircumcised
also? Consider: we say, 'Abraham's faith was counted as
10 righteousness'; in what circumstances was it so counted?
Was he circumcised at the time, or not? He was not yet
11 circumcised, but uncircumcised; and he later received the
symbolic rite of circumcision as the hallmark of the
righteousness which faith had given him when he was still
uncircumcised. Consequently, he is the father of all who
have faith when uncircumcised, so that righteousness is
12 'counted' to them; and at the same time he is the father of
such of the circumcised as do not rely upon their circumcision alone, but also walk in the footprints of the faith
which our father Abraham had while he was yet uncircumcised.

∗ Chapter 4 shows that the teaching on God's justice and man's
justification in 3: 21–6 really fulfils what is in the Old Testament, if it is read with true understanding. Taking Abraham,
the key figure of Judaism, Paul proves that he was justified,
neither because of anything he had done nor because he was
circumcised, but only through faith; therefore it is not necessary for a man to be circumcised if he is to be acceptable to God.

1–2. Paul describes Abraham as *our ancestor in the natural line*.
He must therefore be attempting at this point to answer possible Jewish objections to his teaching. To the Jew *Abraham* was
not only the founder of his race but the great example of faith,
because he was ready to sacrifice his son Isaac at God's command (Gen. 22). So Paul chooses the crucial case of Abraham
and bases his argument on the Old Testament itself, which was
an authority for both himself and the non-Christian Jew. The

46

Jew would have argued that *Abraham was justified* because he obeyed God and was circumcised, and that therefore Abraham and, by implication, the whole Jewish race had *a ground for pride*, which would contradict the conclusion of 3 : 27–8.

3–5. The quotation in verse 3 comes from Gen. 15 : 6; Paul used it also at Gal. 3 : 6. Like Hab. 2 : 4, quoted at 1 : 17, it was a text which allowed Paul to argue that his views were already anticipated in the Old Testament. But why had the Jews not come to Paul's point of view? The Jew understood *faith* in Gen. 15 : 6 as a definite activity on *Abraham's* part—his faithfulness to God's will; it was thus viewed as a form of *righteousness* which Abraham achieved, and Abraham was regarded as measuring up to God's standard—he was 'justified by' something 'he had done' (verse 2). If then God *counted* Abraham as righteous, it was God's response to Abraham's faith. But for Paul *faith* is man's response to what God has done in revealing his justice in the death of Jesus (1 : 17; 3 : 21–6). Paul shows that his interpretation of Gen. 15 : 6 is correct by the way he explains *counted*. If Abraham's faith was the equivalent of righteousness, or a form of righteousness, God would be forced to accept Abraham as righteous, just as *wages* are *paid* in return for work done. But *counted* does not mean 'reckoned as an equivalent' but indicates a *favour* on God's part: that God counts Abraham righteous is an act of his 'free grace alone' (3 : 24), and not a reward for Abraham's faith. Indeed, before God all men are sinners (3 :23) or *guilty*. If God *acquits the guilty* this can only be a *favour*, or act of grace.

In saying that God *acquits the guilty* Paul clearly contradicts both what would normally be expected (that God should condemn the guilty) and the type of behaviour the Old Testament requires from men, who are told not 'to justify the wicked' (Isa. 5 : 23, where the words of the Septuagint are identical with those Paul uses here). The goodness of God, revealed in Jesus, cuts across ordinary ideas of rewards and punishments; man's justification rests on God's 'free grace alone' (3 : 24).

6–8. It was an accepted principle of Jewish interpretation of

Scripture that where the same word occurred in two texts one passage might be used to explain the other. Since Paul also found the word for *counted* in the Septuagint of Ps. 32: 1–2 he can use it to help to elucidate Gen. 15: 6. The Jews would have said that a man was *happy* when his good deeds outweighed his sins; Paul adduces the Psalm to show that a man is happy when his sins are *forgiven*, whether he has any good deeds or not. Forgiveness of sin and the accounting of a man as just are the negative and positive aspects of the same thing. The positive aspect is more important for Paul, and he talks much less about the forgiveness of sin; the latter might suggest that the forgiven man stood in a neutral position between good and evil; the justified man *is* just.

David speaks: in common with the Jews of his day Paul believed that most of the Psalms were written by King David.

9–12. Paul now uses Gen. 15: 6 to illuminate Ps. 32: 1–2 and refute the possible objection that since Ps. 32 was written by a *circumcised* man for *circumcised* Jews, its promise did not apply to the *uncircumcised*. Gen. 15: 6 proves that circumcision was not the cause of Abraham's justification; for the account of Abraham's circumcision (Gen. 17: 1–14) does not precede but follows the story of Gen. 15: 6: the Jewish teachers of Paul's period reckoned the interval between the two events as 29 years. Strictly speaking, therefore, Abraham was not a Jew (in the sense that he practised the Jewish religion) until he had been circumcised, and so Gen. 15: 6 applies to the uncircumcised, as must also Ps. 32: 1–2 because it uses the word *counted*. *Consequently* uncircumcised Abraham is the spiritual *father* of the *uncircumcised* Gentiles who believe, just as circumcised Abraham is the *father* of *circumcised* Jews who believe. Rightly understood, his fatherhood relates not to biological descent but to the faith relationship. Abraham indeed received the command to circumcise himself and his household as the *hallmark*, or recognition, of the already existing righteousness which *faith had given him when he was still uncircumcised*. ✻

ABRAHAM JUSTIFIED NOT THROUGH LAW
BUT THROUGH PROMISE

For it was not through law that Abraham, or his posterity, 13 was given the promise that the world should be his inheritance, but through the righteousness that came from faith. For if those who hold by the law, and they alone, are 14 heirs, then faith is empty and the promise goes for nothing, because law can bring only retribution; but where there is 15 no law there can be no breach of law. The promise was 16 made on the ground of faith, in order that it might be a matter of sheer grace, and that it might be valid for all Abraham's posterity, not only for those who hold by the law, but for those also who have the faith of Abraham. For 17 he is the father of us all, as Scripture says: 'I have appointed you to be father of many nations.' This promise, then, was valid before God, the God in whom he put his faith, the God who makes the dead live and summons things that are not yet in existence as if they already were. When hope 18 seemed hopeless, his faith was such that he became 'father of many nations', in agreement with the words which had been spoken to him: 'Thus shall your posterity be.' With- 19 out any weakening of faith he contemplated his own body, as good as dead (for he was about a hundred years old), and the deadness of Sarah's womb, and never doubted God's 20 promise, but, strong in faith, gave honour to God, in the 21 firm conviction of his power to do what he had promised. And that is why Abraham's faith was 'counted to him as 22 righteousness'.

Those words were written, not for Abraham's sake 23 alone, but for our sake too: it is to be 'counted' in the same 24

way to us who have faith in the God who raised Jesus our
25 Lord from the dead; for he was delivered to death for our
misdeeds, and raised to life to justify us.

* If Abraham was not justified because he had been circumcised, then it might be argued that he was justified because he
kept the law. But Abraham's faith was not based on what he
had done in obeying God but on the promise God had made to
him. He was justified, therefore, by God's goodness, to which
his faith responded. Paul concludes the chapter by asserting that
what was true for Abraham is true for everyone, and that therefore justification is through faith and based on the death and
resurrection of Jesus.

13–15. Gen. 15: 6, of which Paul makes so much use in this
chapter, is preceded by a verse which records a *promise* made by
God to Abraham that his descendants should be as many in
number as the stars. This *promise* is found also in slightly
different forms as made at other stages in Abraham's life
(Gen. 12: 2–3; 17: 4–6; 22: 17–18). The Jews combined the
promises and took them to mean that they, as the *posterity* of
Abraham, would have all *the world* as their *inheritance*. When
Paul speaks here of the *law*, he has in mind the law given to the
Jews hundreds of years later in the time of Moses; therefore the
promise was prior to the *law*. At Gal. 3: 17 Paul uses this priority
of the promise to assert its superiority over the law. It is brought
into the argument here by the words *where there is no law there
can be no breach of law;* there was no law in Abraham's day;
Abraham was not therefore justified through keeping the law.
The relationship of sin to the law, at which Paul here hints, is
expanded in 5: 13–14 and 7: 7–13. However Paul in Romans
emphasizes the fact that the promise is associated in Gen.
15: 5–6 with the *righteousness that came from faith* and therefore
does not depend on the keeping of the *law*. If it is argued that to
hold by the law is the way to inherit, as the Jews would have
argued, then *faith* is denuded of its importance and *the promise*
which accompanied it goes for nothing. To those who *hold by*

it, *the law* can only bring a reward if it is kept and punishment if it is disobeyed. No one does keep the law (3: 9, 19–20, 23), and therefore it *can bring only* retribution. Thus, to attempt to gain the inheritance by obedience to law can only lead to failure.

16–17. A deeper understanding of the nature of *promise* shows that it cannot be associated with the keeping of law. Once the *promise* of an inheritance has been made, there is nothing a man can do to obtain it other than to wait in patient hope for it to be given to him at the death of the testator. He then receives it simply because it has been promised; so its fulfilment is *a matter of sheer grace*, in no way earned by the good behaviour of the one to whom the promise was made. If the promise had been made as a reward for keeping the law, non-Jews would have been automatically excluded, but we have seen (4: 11–12) that *Abraham's posterity* includes both Jewish Christians and Gentile Christians. This is now confirmed from the *promise* itself, for in one of its forms (Gen. 17: 5) God says *I have appointed you to be father of many nations'*, and Paul takes the plural *nations* to include Gentiles as well as Jews. According to the Genesis story (17: 5) the meaning of *Abraham's* name is *father of many nations*. God stood behind *this promise* and therefore it is inviolable; Abraham's *faith* was not of course in the *promise* itself, but in the *God* who made it, and he had good reason to trust him, for he is the God who can make *the dead live* and make promises about *things that are not yet in existence*.

18–22. The description of God at the end of verse 17 is related to what Paul now says about the promise to Abraham. At the time when the promise was made Isaac was 'not yet in existence'; moreover Abraham and Sarah were elderly, being respectively a hundred years old and ninety years old (Gen. 17: 17); as far as the birth of a child was concerned they could be counted *as dead*, and for Isaac to be born would be like making 'the dead live'. Both Abraham and Sarah laughed when they were first told that they should have a child (Gen. 17: 17; 18: 12); their case was *hopeless*. Abraham was well aware of this, for he *contemplated his own body* and also *Sarah's*. Therefore the only possible person in whom to hope was God. *Hope* and *faith* are closely related since both imply dependence on God.

We are given here a new insight into the nature of faith: it is the *firm conviction of* God's *power to do what he* has *promised*. A man who is *strong in faith* is not someone who believes the impossible or who fights a hopeless battle against crushing odds, but the one who leaves it to God to accomplish his purpose and knows that he will, because he is 'the God who makes the dead live and summons things that are not yet in existence as if they already were' (verse 17). Faith is the acceptance of what God has promised, as opposed to the idea of winning something from God by obedience to him or by being good. To accept what God has promised is to *honour* him, since he is then taken to be the kind of God he says he is. To fail to accept his promise is to refuse 'to honour him as God' (1: 21) and so to fall away into sin and to come under his retribution (1: 18). The quotations in verse 18 are from Gen. 17: 5 and 15: 5.

Paul's argument in this chapter appears to depend on the details of certain incidents in the story of Abraham as told in Genesis, namely, Abraham's age and the relative order in which the promise and circumcision took place (verse 10). In 5: 12-21 we shall see that Paul regards Adam as a real historical person though few people today think of him as such. In 9: 25-6 Paul takes a promise which originally applied to a part of Israel and applies it to the Gentiles. In 10: 6-8 he actually applies to the Gospel, as opposed to the Law, a passage which originally referred to the Law.

Is Paul then using the Old Testament in the correct way? For the precise way in which Paul uses the Old Testament at the places mentioned, see the notes on them. More generally we may say that Paul regarded the Old Testament as a book about the coming of the Messiah, and therefore a book about the Gospel. He would have argued, and does so elsewhere, that the Jews of his own day did not properly understand their own book because they did not understand that the Messiah whom it promised had actually come and was Jesus. Looking back at the Old Testament from the position of advantage which faith in Jesus as the Messiah gave, he is able to see much more in the Old Testament than they did. Thus when he points to Abraham as an example of one who was justified through faith, he is pointing to a train of thought which runs all through the Old Testament. It is not a book of law alone; within it there are already indications that God has another way of bringing righteousness to men. We have already seen that to understand Paul's doctrine of righteousness we need to know how the Old Testament used the word (see pp. 15–17). Thus Paul would defend his use of the Old Testament by claiming that he was reinterpreting it in the light of its own deepest and most spiritual thought.

Notice how often he refers to the Old Testament as 'scripture', i.e. as something which stands written and has authority. It is an authority which both he and his Jewish opponents respected; that is why it is mainly when he is arguing with them or explaining their place in God's plan that he explicitly appeals to it. In other parts of Romans he uses it much less frequently, and in some of his letters where he is not dealing with the relationship of Jews and Gentiles he hardly quotes it at all. Yet even when he is not explicitly using it, his thought goes back to it and draws from it again and again. His own most important teaching depends in part on insights into God's ways of working which he learnt from the Old Testament, though he only realized the real truth of the Old Testament after he had come to faith in God through Jesus. His main arguments, however, do not depend on those Old Testament texts which he quotes in a way that we feel is difficult. His doctrine of justification has already been explained, in 3: 21–6, before he brings in the example of Abraham.

23–5. Chapter 4 has not been just a quick survey of the story of Abraham but an examination of the key figure of the Jewish faith in order to show that in his case God did not act along lines of law and retribution but of faith, grace and justification; and what is true for *Abraham* is true for us. Abraham is 'the father of many nations' (verse 17) and so the promise is for all who have faith as he had; righteousness will also be *counted* to them. Abraham believed in the God who 'makes the dead live' (verse 17); we know of a greater 'resurrection' than that of Isaac, for God *raised Jesus our Lord*, in whose *death* we see displayed God's justice (3: 25-6), his way of righting wrong (1: 17). Paul normally speaks of Jesus as dying to justify us (3: 24-6) and the unusual connexion made here between justification and his resurrection probably indicates that Paul is using a piece of early Christian tradition known to the Roman Christians (cf. note on 1: 3-4). This involves no fundamental change in his thought, since the death and resurrection of Jesus are really one event in which God acts for the salvation of men. For the connexion of sin (*misdeeds*) and justification see verses 6-8.

delivered to death may contain an allusion to the 'suffering servant' of Isa. 53 (especially 53: 12) which was taken in the early church as a prophecy of Jesus' suffering.

Thus in chapter 4 we see that Abraham was justified neither through his circumcision nor through his keeping of the law but through his faith, his acceptance of the promise of God. And since the God who dealt with Abraham is our God, having the same power to raise the dead, the way of Abraham's faith is our way, and it is the only way. Thus the principles enunciated in 3: 21-6 are verified in the case of Abraham and reapplied to all men.

Paul has now explained both man's need to be justified because he sins (1: 18 — 3: 20) and how God does in fact justify men through faith by the death of Jesus (3: 21 — 4: 25). He is aware that it will be objected that in this way he has undercut the motive which drives men to be good, since he has made salvation depend on faith and not on obedience to God's will. He has already alluded briefly to this difficulty (3: 7-8) and it must often have been put to him by Jews; it will always arise where Paul's teaching meets a way of life which depends on obedience to a moral standard. In chapters 5–8 Paul sets about answering the difficulty by exploring the nature of the life of the man who is justified by faith (1: 17) and shows that a life which rests on faith in God should not, and indeed does not, lead to immorality but results in goodness. ✳

JUSTIFICATION AND SALVATION

Therefore, now that we have been justified through faith, **5** let us continue at peace with God through our Lord Jesus Christ, through whom we have been allowed to enter the 2 sphere of God's grace, where we now stand. Let us exult in the hope of the divine splendour that is to be ours. More 3 than this: let us even exult in our present sufferings, because we know that suffering trains us to endure, and endurance brings proof that we have stood the test, and this proof is the ground of hope. Such a hope is no mockery, 5 because God's love has flooded our inmost heart through the Holy Spirit he has given us.

For at the very time when we were still powerless, then 6 Christ died for the wicked. Even for a just man one of us 7 would hardly die, though perhaps for a good man one might actually brave death; but Christ died for us while we were yet sinners, and that is God's own proof of his love 8 towards us. And so, since we have now been justified by 9 Christ's sacrificial death, we shall all the more certainly be saved through him from final retribution. For if, when we 10 were God's enemies, we were reconciled to him through the death of his Son, much more, now that we are reconciled, shall we be saved by his life. But that is not all: we 11 also exult in God through our Lord Jesus, through whom we have now been granted reconciliation.

✻ Chapters 5–8 form a new section of the letter; 5: 1–11 is a transition paragraph from the theme of the Christian's justification (3: 21 — 4: 25) to the nature of the new life into which he has entered (5: 12 — 8: 39). In this paragraph the man whom God has justified is seen to be also the man with whom God has made peace; and as such he is assured of salvation in the day of judgement.

1–2. There are two possible ways of translating some of the phrases of these verses: *let us continue at peace* could be 'we are at peace', which the footnote gives as an alternative; similarly the recurring *let us exult* (here and in verse 3) could be 'we exult'. These differences arise because the Greek manuscripts have different forms of the same word. These would have sounded the same in the Greek of Paul's day and therefore either could easily have arisen from the other when manuscripts were being copied by dictation. The form chosen by the N.E.B. belongs to the usually more reliable manuscripts, but we prefer that of the footnote because it is more appropriate to the context. Throughout this passage Paul is making statements about the position of the believer before God rather than exhorting him to some particular activity. If the N.E.B. translation is followed, then it must be understood in the sense: 'Let us enjoy the possession of the peace we have.'

Peace with God is not something we appropriate to ourselves or maintain for ourselves but a gift God has granted us: *therefore* (this word is to be stressed as the link with what has preceded) *now that* a new relationship (*we have been justified*) exists between God and ourselves, we are at *peace with* him. This *peace* is not an inner harmony of mind or a repose of soul but is also itself a relationship to God (cf. verse 10). As our justification was through Jesus' death so also we have our peace *through* him. In *faith* we have responded to God's righteousness and so *we now stand* within *the sphere of God's grace*, i.e. we are where God's love and goodness are able to work on us to produce in us a new kind of life (the theme of 5: 12 — 8: 39); when one human being loves another the life of the second may be entirely changed through the realization that he is loved. Because *we have been justified* we also *exult in the hope of . . . divine splendour*. This *splendour* was lost in sin (see note on 3: 22–3) but will be ours again in the day of judgement; it necessarily follows our justification (cf. 8: 18, 30). Our *hope* is thus no mere hope that something may happen but a sure confidence born of the fact that already *we have been justified*.

3–5. The Christian of Paul's day refused to take part in many of the social and political activities of his time because they were too closely associated with idolatry and immorality; this was a kind of negative *suffering*. Moreover he also went at times in danger of his life and property through sporadic rioting and persecution; those who stand aside from the accepted ways of society are often made its scapegoats when things go wrong. This should not reduce the Christian to fear and misery; instead he will *exult* in *sufferings*. The word Paul uses for *exult* is the one he used at 3: 27 and 4: 2 for 'pride'. 'Pride' in our goodness or achievements is wrong, but there is a legitimate pride 'in the hope of divine splendour' (verse 2), in our *sufferings*, and in what God has done for us through Jesus (verse 11); this pride is not in ourselves but in God. When we have come through *suffering*, *the ground of* our *hope* (what it consists in was defined in verse 2) is ratified. For to pass through *suffering* is to learn a greater dependence on God: faith and *hope* are thus built up. *Such a hope is no mockery* (quoted loosely from Ps. 22: 5, cf. Ps. 25: 3, 20), no self-delusion; in ordinary life hope may make fools of us but this *hope* is assured to us by *the Holy Spirit* (see pp. 89–91) whom God *has given us* and who brings home to us *God's love* for us.

6–8. 'God's love' (verse 5) is not just the assertion that God loves us nor a conviction on our part that this is so: it is *Christ* dying *for the wicked*. Paul emphasizes the nature of those for whom Christ died: they are *powerless* (to do good), *wicked*, *sinners*, 'God's enemies' (verse 10). It is beyond human expectation that anyone should die for people like that. Men have, of course, died for others; half-way through verse 7 Paul appears to realize this and, as it were, pauses in his dictation to correct the first half with *for a good man one might actually brave death*. If there is any distinction between a *just man* and a *good man*, the former is the strict and upright man and the latter the man of warm compassion. In the eyes of one man another may appear so good that he is willing to die for him, but from God's point of view there are no men who are good, all are *wicked*. Thus those for whom Jesus died were *wicked*; there was nothing attractive in them to call out God's love. Jesus' death is then *God's own proof of his love towards us*, the essential way in which God shows his love for men.

9–11. We return again to our starting point—*we have now been justified*. What does this imply for the ultimate future—the day of judgement? *We shall . . . certainly be saved*. Justification belongs to the present, salvation to the future, but the former ensures the latter. Verse 10 reiterates verse 9 by the use of a new metaphor—the reconciliation of enemies—which was already implicit in verse 1 ('at peace with God'). Once we *were God's enemies*; this does not mean that God was our enemy, for Paul has already clearly proved (verses 6–8) God's love for us *through the death of his Son*, but that in our sin we acted in a hostile way towards him. Being his enemies we could not *reconcile* ourselves to him, but he has *reconciled* us to himself by *the death of his Son*. So we are at peace with him. Thus reconciliation and justification are two aspects of God's loving action in Christ, and both bring salvation, 'the hope of the divine splendour that is to be ours' (verse 2). Reference is made to both the *death* and the *life* of Jesus. The latter means Jesus' risen life. For Paul the death and the resurrection of Jesus are one event and we should not read too much into the distinction he makes here. Since, however, he is going on to deal with the life of the believer (5: 12 ff.), it is only natural that he should refer now to the life of Jesus, on whose risen life the new life of the believer depends. In the final verse Paul again breaks forth into praise at the wonderful *reconciliation* which is ours by God's action in *our Lord Jesus*. ✳

DEATH AND LIFE

Mark what follows. It was through one man that sin 12
entered the world, and through sin death, and thus death
pervaded the whole human race, inasmuch as all men have
sinned. For sin was already in the world before there was 13
law, though in the absence of law no reckoning is kept of
sin. But death held sway from Adam to Moses, even over 14
those who had not sinned as Adam did, by disobeying a
direct command—and Adam foreshadows the Man who
was to come.

But God's act of grace is out of all proportion to Adam's 15
wrongdoing. For if the wrongdoing of that one man
brought death upon so many, its effect is vastly exceeded
by the grace of God and the gift that came to so many by
the grace of the one man, Jesus Christ. And again, the gift 16
of God is not to be compared in its effect with that one
man's sin; for the judicial action, following upon the one
offence, issued in a verdict of condemnation, but the act of
grace, following upon so many misdeeds, issued in a verdict of acquittal. For if by the wrongdoing of that one man 17
death established its reign, through a single sinner, much
more shall those who receive in far greater measure God's
grace and his gift of righteousness, live and reign through
the one man, Jesus Christ.

It follows then, that as the issue of one misdeed was 18
condemnation for all men, so the issue of one just act is
acquittal and life for all men. For as through the disobedi- 19
ence of the one man the many were made sinners, so
through the obedience of the one man the many will be
made righteous.

20   Law intruded into this process to multiply law-breaking.
    But where sin was thus multiplied, grace immeasurably
21 exceeded it, in order that, as sin established its reign by way
    of death, so God's grace might establish its reign in right-
    eousness, and issue in eternal life through Jesus Christ our
    Lord.

✻ Paul continues to explore the position of the man who has
been justified. Such a man 'gains life' (1: 17). Then what about
the death that claims everyone? Does this not make a mockery
of 'life?' By comparing and contrasting Adam and Jesus, Paul
shows that the life which comes through Jesus is more powerful
than the death which came through Adam, and so there is indeed new life for the man who is justified.

    12. Paul has already argued that there is no 'distinction' be-
tween the Jew and the Gentile, 'for all alike have sinned' (3:
22–3). There can be no distinction because both are descended
from Adam (for Paul's view of Adam, see pp. 61 f.), and it
was because Adam disobeyed God in eating the fruit which
God had forbidden him to eat (Gen. 3) *that sin entered the world*
and obtained a grip on all men. This sin of Adam was the first
sin of all, and once it had entered no one was able to escape its
power; just as a child picks up the words and gestures of those
among whom it is reared, so it picks up the sin that is already
in the world. Thus though *all men have* indeed *sinned* by their
own personal acts, these sins cannot be dissociated from the *sin*
that *entered the world* when Adam disobeyed. No one can ever
be back in the position of Adam when there was no sin in the
world and so be unaffected by the sin of Adam.

    While, then, we are responsible for our own sins and not
guilty because Adam sinned, yet we do not just copy Adam
in his sin but are predisposed to sin because he brought sin
into the world. And because the punishment for Adam's sin
was *death*, and *inasmuch as all men have sinned, death* has *pervaded
the whole human race* and all men die. When Paul speaks of *death*

he means much more than the end of physical life; throughout this passage death is contrasted with that life by which Paul means spiritual or eternal life (verse 21), a new kind of life which he gradually explains through chapters 5–8. Death, however, brings a man to judgement and, since all men have sinned, therefore to condemnation and punishment by God; and Paul has all this in mind when he speaks of death.

The connexion between the death of men and the sin and death of Adam had already been taught among the Jews prior to Paul, but it does not appear in the Old Testament outside Gen. 3. The Old Testament was more concerned to emphasize the fact that men did sin than to explain why they sinned. The Jews of Paul's day often spoke of Adam, the first man, as 'the man'. They could do this because the word 'Adam' in Hebrew also means 'man'; it is the word used in Gen. 1 for 'man' before the particular man 'Adam' is mentioned in Gen. 3. Paul is able to take up this idea that Adam is 'the man' and use it because Jesus had also called himself 'the man'. The title 'the Son of Man', which Jesus often gave himself (Mark 2: 10; 8: 31; 10: 45; 14: 62, etc.), meant 'the man' in the Aramaic language which Jesus spoke in his daily life. There was thus a comparison ready to hand between Adam and Jesus, and it is this which Paul develops in this passage and which he also uses in 1 Cor. 15: 20–3, 45–9. This comparison is also related to the Jewish belief about the two Ages (see pp. 41 f.). In the Old Age, of which Adam is typical, there is sin and death: in the New Age, which was to come with the Messiah, there would be life and righteousness. Since the Messiah, i.e. Jesus, has already come, there is even now life and righteousness for those who have faith in God through him.

While people no longer generally think of Adam as a historical person who lived 6,000 or so years ago and from whom the whole human race is biologically descended, Paul did; however, his argument does not ultimately depend on this. Without believing in an actual Adam we can accept Paul's thesis that all men are caught together in sin because they have been born into a world in which there is sin; in that sense 'Adam' represents them. This does not mean that sin is passed on by sexual generation, nor that the latter is inherently sinful. Later in the passage we shall see that Paul connects the believer to Jesus in the same way that he regards all men as connected to Adam. If sin was passed on in the world by the physical process of conception and birth the parallel would not hold.

13-14. These verses are really a parenthesis in which Paul meets an objection; the thought of verse 12 is taken up again in verses 18-19. If *sin* really only exists where there is a *law* to break (cf. 4: 15), and if the law was not given until the time of Moses, what of the period *from Adam to Moses*? People certainly died during that period and so there must have been sin, even though that sin was not reckoned up to be dealt with in a later day of judgement. Death in this period was due, then, not to men's sin but to Adam's disobedience. Therefore when we come to talk about salvation the really important figure is not Moses to whom the law was given but Adam who sinned— *and Adam foreshadows the Man who was to come*. We have now come to the comparison between Adam and Jesus which dominates the passage. Note that Jesus is called 'the one who is to come' at Matt. 11: 3, Heb. 10: 37, and this may well have been a title by which the early Christians knew him.

15-17. As soon as Paul begins to draw out the comparison between Adam and Jesus it breaks down, and he is led to contrast them—for what happens through Jesus far exceeds what happened through Adam. By his act of disobedient *wrongdoing* Adam brought death to men; Jesus obeyed God and life overflows to men. For Jesus' action was more than obedience: it was *God's act of grace*. Note how often *gift* and *grace* are mentioned in these verses. To men who had committed *so many misdeeds* this *act of grace* is the wholly undeserved goodness of God seen in the Cross (5: 6-10). Death as a punishment is meted out, as it were, according to a fixed scale. Grace by its very nature cannot be measured out according to a scale; if it was it would be a reward and thus would not really be showing God's love. Indeed it superabounds and *its effect vastly* exceeds that of Adam's sin; the latter was only a solitary *offence*, but grace overcomes the effect of *many misdeeds*.

But what is *the gift that* comes *to so many?* Paul might have described it straightforwardly as 'life' and completed the contrast of verse 17 by writing 'life establishes its' *reign through the one man, Jesus Christ*; he refrains from this because 'life' by its very nature does not tyrannize over men as death does. So he says that those who receive the gift themselves *shall . . . live and reign.* The future tense should not lead us to think that Paul has primarily in mind life after death, or after the day of judgement, but rather the new life which men enter into now, the life with which chapters 5–8 deal. For the moment we learn that it is freedom from death—not that the believer will not die physically, but that he is freed from death thought of as that which punishes sin and brings men to judgement. The believer will *live* now and for ever in triumph over the death which would like to *establish its reign* over him.

But how does *God's act of grace* enable the believer to *live and reign?* We are helped to understand this by a second contrast which is drawn in the passage—between the *one man* (either Adam or Jesus) and the *many* (all men). 'The *many*' is a Jewish idiom for 'all'; thus Mark 10: 45 should be taken to mean that Jesus 'surrendered his life as a ransom' for all. The equivalence of the two terms 'the many' and 'all' is seen when we compare verses 15–17, 19 with verses 12, 18. The *one man* Adam represents or typifies all men as subject to death: the *one man* Jesus Christ represents or typifies them as open to receive life. 'Inasmuch as all men have sinned' (verse 12) all are subject to death, but inasmuch as all do not have faith all do not receive life.

The Jew took very seriously the way in which human lives are interrelated, so that what happens to one man may affect others; the lives of men are tied together by the very fact that they live together. Thus when Achan stole some of the booty at the fall of Jericho not only was he punished but also his wife and family (Joshua 7); all were counted guilty. So when Adam, the father of mankind, disobeyed, all men were bound to be affected. Equally when Jesus, the Son of God, obeyed, all men would be affected; but, if they refused to accept the gracious *gift of God*, the effect might never appear in their lives and they would not *live and reign*. With Jesus there begins a new humanity which is not subject to the condemnation of death but already lives in the New Age. This togetherness of the new humanity dependent on Jesus reappears throughout the letter.

18–19. *It follows then*: Paul reiterates what he has been saying and makes explicit the comparison between Adam and Jesus. Though Paul says that *through the disobedience* of Adam all *were made sinners* we cannot deduce from that, as has often been wrongly done, that all are guilty because Adam sinned (cf. verse 13).

acquittal and life: Paul is continually moving from the fact that God rights wrong to the *life* which those who have been put in the right (acquitted) gain through faith (1: 17). If God terms a man innocent or acquits him, then that man is innocent, i.e., he is made righteous (cf. on 3: 24), just as he now enjoys the new *life*. As in verse 17, the future tense *will be made righteous* does not need to be taken as a reference to the end of the world; it denotes a present and future life as compared with a past death and implies that it logically follows from the obedience of Jesus; cf. 7: 3 for another similar future tense. The righteousness of the man whom God acquits will become obvious to all at the Day of Judgement when God judges men at the end of the world.

20–1. To Jews the great event in history between Adam and the coming of the Messiah was God's gift to his nation of the *law*, by obedience to which the Jew believed he received *life*. Paul ignores the fact that God gave the law, and says that it *intruded* (in Gal. 3: 19 he says it was given by angels). Its purpose was not to give life but to define *law-breaking* and therefore to *multiply* it (cf. 3: 20; 4: 15; 5: 13). The law reveals sin and against its background *grace* is all the more visible as grace, in that it *immeasurably exceeds* sin. We have again the close association of *righteousness* and *life* (life and *eternal life* are identical in this passage); both depend on God's gracious action in Jesus who 'died for the wicked' (verse 6); the presupposition of *life* is *righteousness*, God's righteousness making man righteous (verse 19). *

NEW LIFE FROM DEATH

What are we to say, then? Shall we persist in sin, so that **6** there may be all the more grace? No, no! We died to sin: 2 how can we live in it any longer? Have you forgotten that 3 when we were baptized into union with Christ Jesus we were baptized into his death? By baptism we were buried 4 with him, and lay dead, in order that, as Christ was raised from the dead in the splendour of the Father, so also we might set our feet upon the new path of life.

For if we have become incorporate with him in a death 5 like his, we shall also be one with him in a resurrection like his. We know that the man we once were has been crucified 6 with Christ, for the destruction of the sinful self, so that we may no longer be the slaves of sin, since a dead man is no 7 longer answerable for his sin. But if we thus died with 8 Christ, we believe that we shall also come to life with him. We know that Christ, once raised from the dead, is never 9 to die again: he is no longer under the dominion of death. For in dying as he died, he died to sin, once for all, and in 10 living as he lives, he lives to God. In the same way you must 11 regard yourselves as dead to sin and alive to God, in union with Christ Jesus.

So sin must no longer reign in your mortal body, exact- 12 ing obedience to the body's desires. You must no longer 13 put its several parts at sin's disposal, as implements for do- ing wrong. No: put yourselves at the disposal of God, as dead men raised to life; yield your bodies to him as

14 implements for doing right; for sin shall no longer be
your master, because you are no longer under law, but
under the grace of God.

✻ The objection is raised that Paul's teaching on justification
would lead men to immorality rather than to do God's will.
Paul argues on the contrary that the believer enters a new life at
his baptism, passing from a life which is dead to God to one
which is alive to him; on the basis of the existence of this new
life he exhorts the believer to obey God in his behaviour. God's
free grace in the acquitting of guilty men will not then lead a
man to sin but into a new life of righteousness.

1–2. Some people had apparently taken statements like
5: 20 to mean that since God's true greatness was seen when in
his *grace* he forgave sins, Paul was unwittingly implying that
men should *sin* so that God's greatness might be seen all the
more (cf. 3: 8, 31 for somewhat similar objections). Paul
utterly repudiates any such implication. He takes up again the
contrast between life and death which he had used in 5: 12–21
in connexion with Jesus and Adam, and applies it now in a
different way. Through Jesus the believer has life in the New
Age; therefore he must have passed out of the Old Age where
death reigned (see note on 5: 12–21). But in order to enter the
New Age a man must die; then only can he rise to a new life in
which he will serve God and in which sin will have no claim on
him. Put loosely, the new life would be life beyond the grave
with God. If, then, the believer now possesses new life as a
member of the new humanity dependent on Jesus (see pp. 63 f.),
he must have already died and escaped sin's claim on him. It is
this which Paul claims when he says: *We died to sin*.

3–4. But how did this death of the believer and his entrance
into *the new path of life* take place? In explanation Paul makes use
of teaching about baptism which must have formed part of the
instruction of new converts and which he now recalls to their
minds (*Have you forgotten?*). There is a certain superficial re-
semblance between death and baptism by immersion; going

down under the water would suggest burial in the ground and coming up out of it emergence from the tomb, i.e. resurrection. So Jesus died, was buried and rose from the tomb, and the believer in his baptism may be said to die, be *buried* and rise again with Jesus. This teaching does not depend on the way baptism is carried out, for Paul sometimes states it without any reference to baptism at all: 'one man died for all and therefore all mankind has died... When anyone is united to Christ, there is a new world' (2 Cor. 5: 14, 17). The imagery of baptism provides a useful illustration to drive it home; we should remember that for Paul there were no Christians who had not been baptized—the convert who accepted God's justification was immediately baptized. To be justified was to enter the New Age, and so baptism was the rite of entry into the New Age.

In 5: 12-21 we have already seen that believers form with Jesus a new humanity; at the moment they accepted by faith God's justification they *were baptized into union with Christ Jesus.* Earlier they had been united with the head of the old humanity, Adam; and his disobedience had affected them all so that they were subject to sin and death. Now they are affected by what the head of the new humanity, Jesus, has done in obedience. In obedience to his Father he had died, been *buried* and had been *raised from the dead.* So his followers are said to have died (or 'been crucified', verse 6) and been *buried with him* and will 'also come to life with him' (verse 8). In union with him they pass through the crucial events of his existence: his death, burial, and resurrection. When the new convert is baptized, he does not act out the death and resurrection of Jesus by going below the water and coming up out of it again in imitation of burial and resurrection and so achieve the new life by his imitation of Jesus. Rather, when Jesus was crucified the old humanity was crucified with him (verse 6) and when a man in faith accepts God's justification and offers himself for baptism this is his appropriation of what Christ has done—his acceptance of it as done for himself. As a result his *feet* are *set ... upon the new path of life.*

67

Sometimes this passage is explained in terms of some of the religions of Paul's day, called the Mystery Religions. The details of these are not too well known, but they appear to have centred on a saviour-god who, like the annual death and re-birth of vegetation in winter and spring, died and rose again. This was believed to happen to the god each year; the new believer would participate in its celebration so that he too died and was reborn. Paul, however, does not make his teaching dependent on the continually repeated experience of such a god, but on a 'once for all' (verse 10) dying and rising of Jesus which had happened as a historical event of the recent past. The explanation given at 5: 12–21 in terms of humanity as united to Adam or Christ seems sufficient to cover the facts also in this passage.

5–7. These verses carry on the thought of verses 3–4. The new humanity is sometimes described as 'the Body of Christ' (cf. 12: 4–5, where the idea is present, if not the exact phrase; see also 1 Cor. 12: 12–27; Col. 1: 18), and the Greek word which lies behind *incorporate* is used of two things which belong to the same organism or body. So the believer belongs to the body of Christ and shares in what happened to that body—death, burial, and resurrection. In verse 4 Paul said that the believer has already set his 'feet upon the new path of life'; here he implies that the fullness of that life is received only at the general resurrection when he will *be one with* Jesus *in a resurrection like his*. While the believer lives in this world the new life of the New Age only begins to appear; when the Old Age has completely disappeared then the new life will be completely realized. *The man we once were* is the man of the Old Age, of the 'Adam humanity', the man who was made a sinner (5: 19); this man is caught by sin and made its *slave*. But when the believer becomes a member of the new humanity his *sinful self* is destroyed and he is set free from sin. This happens because *a dead man* cannot be called to account *for his sin*. The believer is the *dead man* because he has died (*been crucified*) with Jesus. He will not be called to account for his sins, because he has already been justified through faith, i.e. acquitted of them through the death of Jesus (3: 25–6). Thus justification and death with Christ are brought closely together.

The man who dies with Jesus does not merely have his sins forgiven, but is actually delivered from the power of *sin*: he is no longer its *slave* (verse 6). This should not be understood to mean that the believer never sins. Sin is regarded here as a hostile power waging war on man (cf. on 3: 9); in verses 12–14 it is depicted as ruling over him. What Paul means is that the believer is freed from the power of sin, not that he is sinless. As a member of the old humanity he could not escape the rule of sin; now he may, and Paul, therefore, can go on in verses 11–14 to exhort him to avoid actual sins. Since he still lives in this world where sin has its power he cannot escape its pervasive influence but has to fight it; this he is able to do (unlike those depicted in 1: 18 — 3: 20) because his feet are 'set ... upon the new path of life' (verse 4). The believer may still sin, but he is no longer sin's *slave*; he is the slave of Jesus (cf. verses 15–23) and should obey him.

8–10. Whereas verses 5–7 emphasized death, these verses emphasize life. Verse 9 is their core—the resurrection of Jesus. This is a past fact of which there can be no doubt; and Paul and his readers *know* it. Because of Adam's sin all are *under* the rule or *dominion of death*; Jesus, however, has escaped that *dominion* because he is alive after death. No one can die twice, and so he cannot come under it again. His life is lived at a new level (1: 4) where death does not apply. And for the humanity which is associated with him the same must also be true—that humanity has *died with Christ* and so *will also come to life with him* in the day of resurrection.

We have seen (5: 12–21) that *sin* and *death* are closely connected, and so the death of Jesus must have had a connexion with sin—*he died to sin*. Death could not be the punishment for Jesus' own sin as it was for Adam's (5: 12) because Jesus had not sinned ('Christ was innocent of sin'—2 Cor. 5: 21). Jesus did not, then, die because of his own sin but because of the sin of men, and in order to break its power over them; we have already seen that through the death of Jesus the guilty are justified and their sin expiated (3: 25; 4: 5; 5: 9). But how is the death of Jesus effective in dealing with sin and destroying its power? In another letter Paul argues that the sharing of men with Jesus in his death and resurrection worked also the other way round. As in their togetherness they received his life, so he took their sin: 'God made him one with the sinfulness of men' (2 Cor. 5: 21). So the sins of men pass to Jesus and men are set free from their power; but the sins did not destroy Jesus, for God brought him back to life after the cross. Hence sin did not defeat Jesus and it was defeated for us in his death (see also 8: 3–4). Finally, since Jesus rose from the dead, he *lives*, as always, to serve God.

11. This brings us to the heart of Paul's argument. Jesus 'died to sin' (verse 10); believers died with him; therefore they have 'died to sin' (verse 2). They are no longer 'slaves to sin' (verse 6). This is what they need to remember, for it forms the basis on which they are summoned to action (verses 12–14). *As* does not mean 'as if' but 'as really being'; they are members of the new humanity because they have responded to God's way of righting wrong revealed in Jesus.

12–13. Arguing from the fact of their new life Paul now appeals to them to obey God. They still live in the Old Age in so far as they live on earth at all; this is what the phrase *your mortal body* implies. Sin is therefore still active against them. But they also live in the New Age 'in union with Christ Jesus' (verse 11); because of that, *sin* need *no longer reign*—indeed *must* not—and lead them to follow the *desires* of the *body*. This does not refer to what are often loosely termed 'sins of the flesh', e.g. drunkenness and sexual immorality. (If you want to know what Paul terms the 'sins of the flesh', read Gal. 5: 19–21, which is quoted in the notes on 8: 12–13.) Paul uses the word *body* to mean the self as a person engaged in activity. In verse 6 the word translated 'self' is identical with the word rendered 'body' here; so also in 12: 1. Since all kinds of activity are engaged in by the self, its desires concern everything which a man does, says or thinks. He may choose to use the *parts* of his body for good or evil: he ought to put them *at the disposal of God* for good; and this he can do because God has brought him already into the New Age and he has begun already to enjoy new life.

Thus Paul's teaching on the grace of God does not lead to an injunction to men to 'persist in sin, so that there may be all the more grace' (verse 1), but to an exhortation to serve God; in this way the accusation of verse 1 is refuted. We may note in passing that the very fact that Paul appeals to Christians to put themselves *at the disposal of God* implies that they are not yet perfect or sinless (cf. note on verses 5–7).

14. Paul now reaches his conclusion. Those who raise the objection of verse 1 fear that where God's *law* is put aside (and in 5: 20 Paul has treated it as an intruder) and *grace* alone is emphasized, the result will be a lapse into *sin*; but the very opposite is true—*sin* is *no longer* the *master*. For *grace* has meant that the Christians are 'as dead men raised to life' (verse 13) and only goodness, not evil, can be associated with the new life.

One misunderstanding should be avoided. Paul does not intend to suggest that being baptized by itself brings a man to the new life. For Paul the man who is baptized is always the man who by faith has allowed God to justify him, and who in baptism acknowledges that Jesus has died and risen for him. It is such men who set out 'upon the new path of life' (verse 4). Paul guards against this misunderstanding in 1 Cor. 10: 1–13. Some of the Corinthians appeared to think (perhaps under the influence of the Mystery Religions, cf. p. 68) that because they had been baptized and had taken part in the Communion Service they were sure of salvation; Paul points out that the Israelites at the time of the Exodus had rites which corresponded to baptism and Communion but these did not ensure their salvation; and he instances them as a warning example to the Corinthians. ∗

SLAVES OF RIGHTEOUSNESS

15 What then? Are we to sin, because we are not under law
16 but under grace? Of course not. You know well enough
that if you put yourselves at the disposal of a master, to
obey him, you are slaves of the master whom you obey;
and this is true whether you serve sin, with death as its
17 result; or obedience, with righteousness as its result. But
God be thanked, you, who once were slaves of sin, have
yielded whole-hearted obedience to the pattern of teaching
18 to which you were made subject, and, emancipated from
19 sin, have become slaves of righteousness (to use words that
suit your human weakness)—I mean, as you once yielded
your bodies to the service of impurity and lawlessness,
making for moral anarchy, so now you must yield them to
the service of righteousness, making for a holy life.

20   When you were slaves of sin, you were free from the
21 control of righteousness; and what was the gain? Nothing
but what now makes you ashamed, for the end of that is
22 death. But now, freed from the commands of sin, and
bound to the service of God, your gains are such as make
23 for holiness, and the end is eternal life. For sin pays a wage
and the wage is death, but God gives freely, and his gift is
eternal life, in union with Christ Jesus our Lord.

✻ Paul continues to deal with the problem of 6: 1, but from a
new angle: if law is set aside does this not mean that men will sin
freely? He answers that the Christian has a new master to serve,
namely, God, and because he has been set free from sin he is now
able to offer a new obedience. Contrasting the present Christian
and earlier pre-Christian life of his readers he allows no middle
way between the service of sin and that of righteousness.

15–16. Verse 15 re-expresses the position of the objector of verse 1 in terms of verse 14. If the believer is not subject to the *law* but accepts God's justification offered in his *grace*, does that not necessarily imply that without the constraining power of law and its clear statement of what is right and wrong he will *sin*? Paul again firmly repudiates the implication, arguing that the Christian has a new *master*; the exclusion of the law thus leaves no gap for immorality to enter. He lays down the obvious truth that *slaves* must *obey* their *masters*, and a change of *master* does not mean an end of obedience. For man there are only two possible *masters—sin* or *righteousness*. Throughout the passage he gives varying names to the latter—*obedience*, 'the pattern of teaching' (verse 17), 'the service of God' (verse 22)— but in the final analysis the alternatives are sin or God. (Note that sin appears here again as a power ruling over men; see note on verses 5–7.) Paul probably emphasizes *obedience* at this point because it forms a strong contrast to *sin*, which is disobedience to God.

The transition from the imagery of baptism in verses 1–14 to that of slavery in verses 15 ff. probably follows from the fact that in the early Church converts were said to be baptized 'into the name of Jesus'. In the language of the time, when a man put his name on someone or something he was declaring his ownership of that person or object; thus the baptized convert belonged to Jesus as a *slave* belonged to his *master*. The result of serving *sin* is *death* (cf. 5: 12); this is not just physical death but death as the judgement God proclaims on wrongdoing, and it necessarily involves exclusion from the life of the New Age. The *result* of *obedience* to God is *righteousness*; God has already justified the Christian so that he is righteous (3: 26; 4: 3; 5: 19); when now he obeys God this *righteousness* appears, and on the last day the actual character of the Christian in the New Age will correspond completely to the judgement already spoken in justification, namely that he is righteous.

17–19. *Once ... once ... now.* The pre-Christian condition of the Roman readers and their present condition are strongly contrasted. *God* is to *be thanked* for the change because he has been 'righting wrong' (1: 17): he has *emancipated* them *from sin* and made them *slaves of righteousness* through the death and resurrection of Jesus. *Slaves of righteousness* is an unexpected phrase and in the parenthesis Paul apologizes for it. The non-Christian, whether the Jew with his Law, which 'brings only the consciousness of sin' (3: 20) and multiplies law-breaking (5: 20), or the Gentile with no law to guide him, can only serve sin; but the believer can yield *whole-hearted obedience to* God. He can do this because he has been justified and *emancipated from sin*; standing thus in a new relationship to God (see notes on 1: 16–17 and 3: 23–4) he is able to offer the obedience which God desires. He is now described as *made subject* to a *pattern of teaching*: a *pattern* can be either an example we follow or, as with a rubber stamp, that which makes the pattern. Paul may then be saying that the Christian has either a pattern which he can follow or there is a pattern to which God shapes him, or Paul may have both ideas in mind. In either case the *pattern* will ultimately be the life of Jesus.

In verse 18 the new life is described as itself slavery—*slaves of righteousness*; cf. 'bound to the service of God' (verse 22). There is a sense in which the believer is free; in Gal. 5: 1 Paul says: 'Christ set us free, to be free men'. Freedom is always freedom from something: the believer is free from enslavement to the law and to sin; he is not free from doing God's will. But he is able to bear this bondage because he has been brought into the new relationship to God of the man who has been justified. Paul particularly emphasizes this bondage here in order to meet the objections of those who argue that he teaches men to sin. Yet this bondage does not mean that the Christian's life is irksome; for Paul it is always full of joy (12: 12; 14: 17). Slavery is the lot of man—he is either a slave to sin or to God; there is no third possibility. The difference between these two bondages lies in the end result. In verse 16 this was described as 'death' or 'righteousness'; here (verse 19) as *moral anarchy* or a *holy life*. Where men serve sin without the law the result is the *moral anarchy* of undisciplined behaviour described in 1: 18–32; where they serve it under the guise of obedience to the law, it is the *moral anarchy* of pride and self-righteousness (2: 1 — 3: 8). But for the believer the end result is a *holy life*.

When Paul called his readers 'dedicated people' (1: 7) he used a word which means 'holy'. They are 'holy people' because God has justified them; because they are holy people they have now to live a *holy life* by yielding themselves (= *bodies* as in 6: 12) *to the service of righteousness*. On the basis of what they are —justified, baptized, holy—Paul calls them to holiness. It would be useless to call the unjustified and unbaptized to holiness. A *holy life* is not simply a life which is good and pure, but one which is dedicated to God's ways. It will in consequence be good and pure; but the primary emphasis lies on its separation from men's ways and its association with God.

20–2. The contrast between 'then' and *now* is continued. *Now* they are *ashamed* of what they were, for they see clearly that the condition described in 1: 18 — 3: 20 was 'moral anarchy'. They were satisfied with it then, but not *now*. Apart from their shame at their sin, they now realize that its *end* was *death*. Their lives now display *holiness* and the *end* will be *eternal life*, the life which they have now begun and which will be theirs in full when the Old Age has completely disappeared.

23. A last contrast is introduced. The word which Paul uses for 'slave' can also mean 'a paid servant' and Paul now appears to slip over into this other meaning. The servant of sin is paid— he has earned his pay—and the *wage is death*. The servant of God is given *eternal life*; but it is not a wage, it is a *gift*. He does not merit it, because the best he does falls far short of what God requires; and what he does in obedience to God he is only able to do because he has been freely justified by God through the death of Jesus and has been given new life. *Sin pays* its *wage* of *death* according to the law to the man 'under law'; *God gives* his free *gift* according to grace to the man 'under grace' (verse 15). ✳

75

FREEDOM FROM THE LAW THROUGH CHRIST

7 You cannot be unaware, my friends—I am speaking to those who have some knowledge of law—that a person is
2 subject to the law so long as he is alive, and no longer. For example, a married woman is by law bound to her husband while he lives; but if her husband dies, she is dis-
3 charged from the obligations of the marriage-law. If, therefore, in her husband's lifetime she consorts with another man, she will incur the charge of adultery; but if her husband dies she is free of the law, and she does not com-
4 mit adultery by consorting with another man. So you, my friends, have died to the law by becoming identified with the body of Christ, and accordingly you have found another husband in him who rose from the dead, so that we
5 may bear fruit for God. While we lived on the level of our lower nature, the sinful passions evoked by the law worked
6 in our bodies, to bear fruit for death. But now, having died to that which held us bound, we are discharged from the law, to serve God in a new way, the way of the spirit, in contrast to the old way, the way of a written code.

* In chapter 7 Paul discusses the place of the law. He has shown already that it has some connexion with the sin from which the believer has been freed. Now in 7: 1-6, using the illustration that a woman is set free by her husband's death to marry again, he shows that the believer is free from the law and united to Christ. This is a bridge section, for verse 4 depends on and summarizes chapter 6, verse 5 prepares for 7: 7-25, and verse 6 for 8: 1-17.

1-3. Paul lays down a general principle: *a person is subject to the law so long as he is alive, and no longer*. This is true both in civil and religious law, and would be understood by all his readers.

In verse 4 Paul restricts its application to the law with which he is concerned, that of the Old Testament. In verses 2–3 he chooses a particularly clear example of the principle as an illustration of what he is going to say.

consorts is a verb often suggestive of an evil association in English; on its first occurrence this implication is present, but not at its second, where the woman re-marries in accordance with the law.

4. The illustration does not quite fit what Paul wishes to say: in it the husband dies and the wife is free to marry again; in verse 4 the wife, i.e. the believer (*you ... have died*), dies and then marries again. The main point of the illustration is that through death a person has escaped the *law*, but marriage itself also suggests something of the nature of the relationship between the believer and Christ. We have already seen that baptized believers have died with Christ (6: 1–11); they have *identified* themselves with his death. It is this same death which is also their death *to the law*. *The body of Christ* is the body on the cross (the first half of the verse refers to his death and the second to his resurrection). Perhaps Paul chooses the phrase here because it carries the extra idea, through its reference to the church (see notes on 6: 5–7 and 12: 4–5), of the 'solidarity' or 'togetherness' of believers with Christ; the believer is a 'limb' or 'organ' or Christ (12: 5), a member of the new humanity which is Christ's body. It is the togetherness of believers with Christ in his death which enables Paul to speak of their death. The believer, once dead, is free from the law and has the opportunity of another marriage; as we know already from chapters 5 and 6, his new relationship is with Jesus.

The relationship of the devotee to his god is described in many religions as marriage. We find examples of this in both the Old and New Testaments: Hosea was in his own marriage a symbol of the relation between his people and God (Hos. 1–3); Jeremiah speaks to his people of their 'love as a bride' to God (Jer. 2: 2 as in R.S.V.); in Eph. 5: 25 husbands are told to love their wives 'as Christ also loved the church'. It obviously implies a close personal relationship. In our passage the image is not explored in any way other than to suggest that the purpose of the marriage is to *bear fruit for God*; the activities of the new life of righteousness when the believer is married to Jesus will be like the children of a marriage. Thus, as in chapter 6, Paul ends by indicating the necessity for actual righteousness; though the law has no hold on the Christian, his behaviour does matter.

5-6. Here we have once more the contrast between life prior to faith in Christ and the life of faith (cf. 6: 17-23). The former is lived on *the level of our lower nature*. It is easy to misunderstand this phrase. It recurs repeatedly in 8: 1-17, where it is contrasted with life 'on the level of the spirit' (8: 6). We should misinterpret Paul entirely if we were to think that he was thereby opposing two parts of man's nature, a higher and a lower, and implying that we should live by the higher. To live 'on the level of the spirit' is not natural to man; such life comes into existence only when the believer responds in faith to Jesus, and the Spirit of God begins to produce new life (cf. 8: 11) in him; the phrase is indeed another way of describing the nature of that new life. Those without faith in Jesus inevitably live *on the level of our lower nature*; it is the level described in 1: 18 — 3: 20, where *sinful passions* dominate; it is the level of the old humanity of Adam (5: 12-21). Since it is a life without faith through Jesus, it is a life without God. Whereas the union with Jesus of verse 4 results in a new life of righteousness, these *sinful passions* result in *death*. Note that Paul uses *bear fruit* in both cases.

The Jews believed that *the law* would help men to attain the new life; instead it really *evoked the sinful passions*. How *the law* does this is explained more fully in verses 7-11. *But now* the believer has been freed from *the law* (cf. 6: 14); *sinful passions* will not therefore be awakened by it. The believer is discharged (cf. verse 2) *from the law*, so that it has no claim on his obedience. This does not mean that he has escaped the service of God, but that he serves him in a new way. It is now no longer his aim to make his conduct correspond with the detailed prescriptions of a *written code*, but he has within him a *new* power, *the way of the spirit*, to direct him in God's service. This does not merely mean that the believer has a new ability to keep the law but that he has entered into a new life where the law no longer holds sway. 8: 1–17 explains in detail what that means. ✳

SIN AND THE LAW

What follows? Is the law identical with sin? Of course not. 7 But except through law I should never have become acquainted with sin. For example, I should never have known what it was to covet, if the law had not said, 'Thou shalt not covet.' Through that commandment sin found its 8 opportunity, and produced in me all kinds of wrong desires. In the absence of law, sin is a dead thing. There was a 9 time when, in the absence of law, I was fully alive; but when the commandment came, sin sprang to life and I died. The commandment which should have led to life 10 proved in my experience to lead to death, because sin 11 found its opportunity in the commandment, seduced me, and through the commandment killed me.

Therefore the law is in itself holy, and the command- 12 ment is holy and just and good. Are we to say then that this 13 good thing was the death of me? By no means. It was sin that killed me, and thereby sin exposed its true character: it used a good thing to bring about my death, and so, through the commandment, sin became more sinful than ever.

We know that the law is spiritual; but I am not: I am un- 14 spiritual, the purchased slave of sin. I do not even acknow- 15 ledge my own actions as mine, for what I do is not what I want to do, but what I detest. But if what I do is against my 16 will, it means that I agree with the law and hold it to be

17 admirable. But as things are, it is no longer I who perform
18 the action, but sin that lodges in me. For I know that
nothing good lodges in me—in my unspiritual nature, I
mean—for though the will to do good is there the deed is
19 not. The good which I want to do, I fail to do; but what I
20 do is the wrong which is against my will; and if what I do
is against my will, clearly it is no longer I who am the agent,
but sin that has its lodging in me.

21 　I discover this principle, then: that when I want to do
22 the right, only the wrong is within my reach. In my inmost
23 self I delight in the law of God, but I perceive that there is
in my bodily members a different law, fighting against the
law that my reason approves and making me a prisoner
24 under the law that is in my members, the law of sin. Miser-
able creature that I am, who is there to rescue me out of this
25 body doomed to death? God alone, through Jesus Christ
our Lord! Thanks be to God! In a word then, I myself, subject to God's law as a rational being, am yet, in my unspiritual nature, a slave to the law of sin.

✽ In this section Paul takes up the question which is raised by
7: 5, where he appeared to have spoken harshly about the law
as if it were the cause of sin. This cannot be so, for the law was
given by God. He therefore now examines the relationship of
the law to sin, and in so doing is led into an analysis of man's behaviour when he is confronted by the demand of God for goodness. If man fails, as he does, to meet God's requirements, then
the fault does not lie with the law—or God's demands—but
with man himself and the sin which attacks him.

　7–8. Paul rejects vehemently any suggestion that *the law* is
sinful. *The law*, in the sense of the moral demands of God which
were pinpointed for the Jew in the Ten Commandments, is so
much an integral part of the Old Testament that to consider it

evil would be to disclaim the whole Old Testament and its story of the Jews. Paul cannot do this; as becomes clear in chapters 9–11, the story of the Jews was an essential preparation for the story of Jesus. What then is the purpose of *the law*? From it we learn what is right and wrong and are placed in the position of choosing between them (cf. 3: 20; 5: 13). But since, as we have already seen, all men have sinned (3: 9–20), the law may be said to bring men into the experience of sin—they *become acquainted with sin*.

To illustrate this Paul uses the Tenth Commandment: 'Thou shalt not covet thy neighbour's house, thou shalt not covet thy neighbour's wife, nor his manservant, nor his maidservant, nor his ox, nor his ass, nor any thing that is thy neighbour's' (Exod. 20: 17; cf. Deut. 5: 21). He puts it in the absolute form: *Thou shalt not covet*, thus implying that all coveting is wrong and that the sin is not just to be limited to what is explicitly forbidden in the commandment itself. To *covet* here means to desire for one-self what another has; it does not imply that any action is taken to seize what the other has: the *desire* itself is *wrong*. All men break this commandment. But since it is so natural on man's part to *covet* and since it does not appear to do our neighbour any harm (though in fact it corrupts our good feelings towards him), we should not know our sin *if the law had not said ' Thou shalt not covet'*. The commandment gave *sin its opportunity*. Or, put the other way round, where *the law* does not prescribe behaviour, *sin is a dead* (inactive) *thing*. Throughout 7: 7–11 Paul has in mind the story of the sin of Adam and Eve (Gen. 3); it was the command not to eat of the tree of good and evil (Gen. 2: 17) which evoked the desire in Adam and Eve to eat. Whenever a limit is set on behaviour man seems to be incited to go beyond it; to be told 'Don't!' arouses the desire to 'do'. In that sense the law may be said to *produce* sin.

9–11. As well as the story of Gen. 3 Paul has probably also in mind his experience as a Jewish boy; in a religious ceremony when he was thirteen years old he would have been officially made obedient to the law. Before that time, *in the absence of law*, like Adam and Eve before God's *commandment* to them, he *was fully alive*. Now when he came under the obligation to obey the law, and was held to be fully responsible for his actions to God, *sin sprang to life*, and he *died*. *Death* is both the result of sin (6: 23) and its punishment (5: 12–21; cf. Gen. 2: 17, 'Of the tree of the knowledge of good and evil, thou shalt not eat of it: for in the day that thou eatest thereof thou shalt surely die'; for *death* see note on 5: 12). The Jews expected that the law would bring *life;* instead it brought *death* because *sin found its opportunity* in it to deceive men (cf. Gen. 3: 13, 'The woman said, The serpent beguiled me'). Thus Paul lays the blame here on *sin* (cf. verse 8) and not on the *law*, and so exonerates the *law*.

12–13. Because *sin* is ultimately to blame, *the law is in itself holy*. *The law* and *the commandment* are *holy* because they come from God who is holy; the commandment is *just* because it is the just demand of a just God on men; it is *good* because it sets out what a good God requires. *The law* is the whole religious system of God's demands on men's behaviour; *the commandment* is an individual precept or regulation within the whole. In conclusion the argument of verses 7–11 is summarized: *sin* is at fault. The law *exposed* sin's *true character* by showing that it was disobedience to God and must result in *death*, and so men's sins *became . . . sinful* beyond measure. The law evokes *sin* (7: 5) and then shows how terrible it is.

14–16. *We know*: from what Paul has just written and from what his readers will already have learnt, he and they can agree that *the law is spiritual*. This is not to say that it belongs to a higher or spiritual part of man, but that it mirrors the nature of God. Men should know for themselves that they do not mirror God's nature, for they are the *slaves of sin* (cf. 6: 16–20); an *unspiritual* life is a life on 'the level of our lower nature' (cf. on 7: 5–6). Paul finds himself trapped; on the one hand he acknowledges that what *the law* demands is good, on the other hand he does not do what it demands. Many have analysed themselves and discovered this disharmony between what they think correct and what they actually achieve. Paul, however, is not just concerned with self-analysis; he uses this to uphold the validity of the law—it is *admirable*. It is wrong to think here of man as split into a higher nature which wills the good (note that in verse 18 the 'will to do good' is in the 'unspiritual nature') and a lower nature which drags it down into doing evil. It is Paul who wills and Paul who acts contrary to his will; and Paul is not content to say that the intention to do good is sufficient, for he knows that God demands good actions.

17–18. If then the law is not to blame for sin, what is? It is *sin that lodges in me*. Paul is the 'slave of sin' (verse 14) and sin has obtained its grip on his 'lower' (7: 5) or *unspiritual nature*; this it can do since to live at that level is to live apart from God (see on 7: 5–6). *Sin*, then, appears as a personal power hostile to man (cf. 3: 9, 20; 6: 6, 16–19). Yet in blaming *sin* Paul is not attempting to shirk responsibility for his sins; he continually speaks of himself as failing to do good (7: 15, 16, 19). Somehow, however, he has to explain that what he wishes to do, he does not do: it is he himself who does not do it; though *sin* may appear as a hostile force, the sins are still Paul's.

19–20. Verse 19 repeats verse 15 and verse 20 repeats verse 17.

21–3. Here the preceding argument is summed up, and the law finally cleared of the accusation that it is evil in its very nature. Verse 21 is Paul's conclusion as to his experience; verses 22–3 lay the blame for his failure not on the law but on the sin which has caught him. The *inmost self* and the *reason* are the same: they mean Paul as he responds to, and acknowledges the correctness of, the law of God. The *bodily members* are Paul as he fails to carry out the demands of God in concrete acts of obedience. We should beware again of dividing man into a higher and a lower nature. Paul speaks of the *inmost self* and the *reason* when he describes his approval of the law, for this is a mental judgement; he speaks of the *bodily members* when he obeys *the law of sin*, because it is through the body that all obedience or disobedience is rendered. The *inmost self* and the *reason* are not a higher or more spiritual part of Paul than the *bodily members*; the two sets of terms represent Paul performing different functions, but it is always Paul who so judges or acts. Nor are the *inmost self* and the *reason* Paul's because he is a Christian (cf. 8: 6); all men have them (cf. 2: 14-16). *The law of sin* is the *principle* by which Paul finds his life governed in verse 21.

24. From this plight the law cannot *rescue* Paul. Indeed it is the law that has created the problem, for, if there had been no law, there would have been no sin (7: 9), and if there had been no sin, there would be no death as its punishment (5: 12; 7: 9, 11). The *body* means Paul as belonging to this world, called to obey the law in concrete acts of obedience (see on 6: 12-13); because of his failure to do so it is *doomed to death*. Paul is trapped in the Old Age under sin's power; only outside help can save and bring him into the New Age; and the outside help is not the law.

25. The first half of this verse answers verse 24: 'rescue' comes from *God alone, through Jesus Christ our Lord*. Chapter 8 takes up and enlarges what this means. The second half of the verse appears to go back on what has just been said as if the 'rescue' had been ineffective. Some scholars have thought it misplaced and have inserted it between verses 23 and 24. There is no evidence in any manuscript that its place is other than where we have it. It is a summary of the argument of verses 7-24 which is to be fully answered in chapter 8. We have a long statement of the problem (7: 7-24); a short statement of the answer (first half of verse 25); a short restatement of the problem (second half of verse 25); a long statement of the answer (chapter 8).

There is one question with which we have not yet dealt directly: of whom is Paul speaking in 7: 7-25? This divides into two questions.

(*a*) Does the first person singular indicate that he speaks of himself alone, or is it a literary device used to suggest all men? The passage is so personal in tone that it appears impossible to exclude Paul's own experience, but he formulates his experience in general terms (e.g. in 7: 7-13 in the terms of the story of the sin of Adam and Eve in Gen. 3); thus what he writes is true not for himself alone but for others, and his use of Gen. 3 indicates that he regards it as true of all men.

(*b*) Was the experience of which Paul writes in 7: 14–25 true of himself (and others) before he became a Christian or does it apply to his life as a Christian? We cannot deny that what Paul describes here can be the experience of a non-Christian, for men who were never affected by Christianity (like the Roman poet Ovid who lived just prior to Jesus) have recorded the same inability to perform the good of which their minds approved. Further, there are no direct references in 7: 14–25 to Jesus or the Spirit such as we would expect if it is an account of a Christian experience (chapters 6 and 8, where Paul definitely describes the Christian life, abound with such references); and 6: 15–23 describes a situation in which sin appears to have lost its power and should therefore be no longer able to dominate the Christian in the way 7: 7–25 depicts. But there are also strong arguments on the other side. From verse 14 onwards Paul writes in the present tense as if describing an experience which was still a present reality to him. There are indications elsewhere in Paul of an inward struggle similar to this which he underwent as a Christian: 'That [lower] nature sets its desires against the Spirit, while the Spirit fights against it. They are in conflict with one another so that what you will to do you cannot do' (Gal. 5: 17). The remainder of the section, chapters 5–8, describes the life of the Christian, and a digression into an earlier period of his life would appear to require a clearer indication of change. The majority of those scholars who hold that 7: 7–25 refers only to Paul's pre-Christian experience find it necessary to transfer the second half of verse 25 to follow verse 23, since in its present position it appears to take back what has been said in the first half to be true for the Christian. Finally we should note that many good Christians (e.g. Augustine, Calvin, Luther) have been happy to accept these verses as a description of Christian experience.

It seems then that readers of the passage have been able to

apply it both to pre-Christian and to Christian experience, and Paul may have left its application vague because it does apply to both. It obviously applies to the non-Christian, but in saying this we need to remember that Paul writes about non-Christian experience from the point of view of a Christian looking back. Not every non-Christian will feel this tension between moral demand and actual performance; it may only be as a Christian that he will become aware how strong is the power of the 'lower nature'. If Paul writes here of the law, it is because that was the way in which God's will presented itself to him as a Jew, but the problem appears whenever an active conscience is faced with a moral demand and it therefore catches others than Jews.

Christians also feel at times this difference between what they accept as God's will (i.e. the law) and what they accomplish in response to it. The footnote in the N.E.B. renders the last half of verse 25 as 'Thus, left to myself, while subject to God's law as a rational being, I am yet in my unspiritual nature, a slave to the law of sin'. 'Left to myself' brings out correctly the strong personal pronoun which is used here in the Greek. Strictly speaking, the Christian is never left to himself by God, but he often cuts himself off from God, and then he finds himself in this situation. So long as he lives in the body, he may unfortunately live at 'the level of the lower nature'; he ought to display the righteousness which is his from God, but often he fails to do so. He belongs to this present evil Old Age and also to the New Age; when he allows himself to slip back into the former and no longer regards himself as dead to sin and alive to God (6: 11), then the law begins again to rule him and sin rules through the law. He ought to put himself at the disposal of God, but does not always do so (6: 13). However, 'the conclusion [a conclusion drawn from the earlier parts of the letter] of the matter is this: there is no condemnation' for him (8: 1). He has believed, and ultimately he will be rescued 'out of this body doomed to death' (7: 24; cf. 8: 23). ✳

THE SPIRIT IS LIFE

The conclusion of the matter is this: there is no condemna- **8** tion for those who are united with Christ Jesus, because in 2 Christ Jesus the life-giving law of the Spirit has set you free from the law of sin and death. What the law could never 3 do, because our lower nature robbed it of all potency, God has done: by sending his own Son in a form like that of our own sinful nature, and as a sacrifice for sin, he has passed judgement against sin within that very nature, so that the 4 commandment of the law may find fulfilment in us, whose conduct, no longer under the control of our lower nature, is directed by the Spirit.

Those who live on the level of our lower nature have 5 their outlook formed by it, and that spells death; but those 6 who live on the level of the spirit have the spiritual out-look, and that is life and peace. For the outlook of the 7 lower nature is enmity with God; it is not subject to the law of God; indeed it cannot be: those who live on such a 8 level cannot possibly please God.

But that is not how you live. You are on the spiritual 9 level, if only God's Spirit dwells within you; and if a man does not possess the Spirit of Christ, he is no Christian. But 10 if Christ is dwelling within you, then although the body is a dead thing because you sinned, yet the spirit is life itself because you have been justified. Moreover, if the Spirit of 11 him who raised Jesus from the dead dwells within you, then the God who raised Christ Jesus from the dead will also give new life to your mortal bodies through his in-dwelling Spirit.

✻ Paul now describes the Christian's existence in a new way by means of a contrast, hinted at in 7: 6, between his lower nature and the Spirit of God. After summarizing the argument of the preceding chapters and affirming the defeat of sin by the death of Jesus (verses 1–4), he shows how the Christian has entered into a new sphere of life created by the presence of the Spirit in him.

1–2. Paul draws a *conclusion* from the earlier chapters. In 5: 16, 18 *condemnation* was set in contrast to 'acquittal'; because the believer has been justified he cannot be condemned by the law. As we have seen in 6: 1–11, he is *united with Christ Jesus*, and so has already passed through *death* which is the punishment for *sin*; so, again, there can be *no condemnation*. And even if as a Christian he has sinned (7: 14–25), this *conclusion* remains true. Making use of the idea of the two laws (7: 23), Paul says that it is true also because the Spirit which gives *life* (that which is opposed to judgement and death) *has set* him *free* from the *sin* which perverts the *law* and results in *death* (cf. 7: 4–6). And this has taken place on the basis of the life, death and resurrection of Jesus Christ. *United with Christ Jesus* is another way of expressing the same circle of ideas which we found in 5: 12–21; 6: 3–4; those *united with Christ Jesus* belong to the new humanity whose head is Jesus; what has happened to him in death and resurrection has affected their lives.

3–4. The *law could never* give us life because our sin always forces it to condemn us. But God has given us life by the *sending* of *his own Son*. Paul emphasizes that our changed condition goes back ultimately to what happened to God's *Son* Jesus. But how? We notice first that there is a certain vagueness about the words *in a form like that of our own sinful nature*. On the one hand Paul wishes to say that in every respect Jesus, God's Son, resembled us with the same lower nature that we have; yet he does not wish to say that he lived 'on the level of our lower nature' (7: 5 and note), for this would imply that he sinned. Sin exercises its power through the lower nature (7: 14–25), and it is there that it must be defeated. If then Jesus is to defeat sin he must defeat it in the lower nature, and therefore he must have one. When he did so defeat it, he did this as the head of the new humanity, and therefore defeated it for all who are in that new humanity and have a lower nature. We move in the same circle of ideas as 5: 15–17; 6: 3–4, where the actions of Jesus as the head of a new humanity are effective for all in that humanity (see in particular the quotations from 2 Cor. 5: 21 on pp. 69–70). A defeat then for sin in Jesus' lower nature was a defeat for sin all along the line, i.e. in lower nature as a whole.

The crucial moment in the battle against sin was the death of Jesus (*a sacrifice*), just as it was in justification and salvation (3: 25; 5: 6–10). For it is in the death of Jesus that his lower nature is seen to have been completely real; the one event which is shared by all who have the lower nature is death, and Jesus was not a divine being who put on the disguise of a lower nature which he could drop at the terrifying moment of death (for crucifixion is terrifying) and evade it. Death was the moment of greatest temptation; a few hours before his death he prayed vehemently to escape it but accepted it as God's will (Mark 14: 32–42). Death was the most likely moment for him to sin and fail; but he did not fail. Thus it was that in dying he triumphed over the flesh and defeated sin completely. In consequence *sin* (and not the sinner) was condemned *within that very* [lower] *nature*. Because this means that sin has been condemned within our lower nature, Paul speaks of *the commandment of the law* as finding *fulfilment in us*. Paul does not say that because we have the Spirit to help us 'we are now able to fulfil the actual commandments of the law'. He says that the *commandment* is fulfilled *in us*, i.e. its requirement has been met because sin has been condemned and because 'there is no condemnation for those who are united with Christ Jesus' (verse 1). 'Those who are united with Christ Jesus' are indeed those *whose conduct ... is directed by the Spirit* (cf. verse 9). This is a new way of defining what a believer is and it is continued in verses 5–8.

Before we examine those verses it is necessary to say a little about *the Spirit* to which Paul refers so much. This Spirit is not man's spirit, a part of his make-up like his body or his mind. It is the Spirit of God or the Spirit of Christ (8: 9); it is often called the Holy Spirit (9: 1; 1: 4). Every man has a human spirit, but Paul regards the Spirit of God as active only in believers, and thereby forming their outlook (8: 5–6). Each Christian has his own human spirit, but when he is said to be 'spiritual' (8: 6) this means that his life is being shaped and determined by God through God's Spirit. Naturally, since the Spirit comes from God, God will form the outlook of the believer in accordance with his (God's) own outlook. Thus the qualities of character which are attributed to God are the qualities which should appear in the Christian life. What the Spirit produces in the believer 'is love, joy, peace, patience, kindness, goodness, fidelity, gentleness, and self-control' (Gal. 5: 22; cf. Rom. 15: 30; 14: 17; 5: 5). These, of course, are also the qualities which distinguished the earthly life of Jesus, and so the Spirit may also be called the Spirit of Christ.

Already in the Old Testament the Spirit had been viewed as leading many of its great men to perform heroic deeds, and the Messiah expected by the Jews was to be specially endowed with the Spirit's help. Isa. 11: 1–2 was taken as a prophecy of this: 'And there shall come forth a shoot out of the stock of Jesse, and a branch out of his roots shall bear fruit: and the spirit of the Lord shall rest upon him, the spirit of wisdom and understanding, the spirit of counsel and might, the spirit of knowledge and of the fear of the Lord.' Following on from this, the New Testament sees the activities of Christians in God's service as the result of the Spirit's work: the activities which Paul lists in Rom. 12: 6–8 are ascribed in 1 Cor. 12 to the work of the Spirit in believers. Indeed the whole life of the believer and of the Church is a life directed, inspired and empowered by the Spirit. This is especially clear in Acts, where the Spirit guides the Church in every important decision. For instance, when Paul and Barnabas were first sent out as missionaries it was because 'the Holy Spirit said, "Set Barnabas and Saul apart for

me, to do the work to which I have called them"' (Acts
13: 2; cf. Acts 11: 12; 16: 6–10).

The exact relationship of the Spirit to God and Christ is
not worked out by Paul. Later Christian theology formulated
the doctrine of the Trinity: One God in three Persons, Father,
Son, and Holy Spirit. While the germ of this is present in Paul's
writing, it is not explicit. The Spirit is certainly distinguished
from God the Father by being called 'God's Spirit' (8: 9; cf.
8: 14–16), and from God the Son by being called 'the Spirit of
Christ' (8: 9); in neither case is the relationship like that of a
man's spirit to himself. Rather the Spirit is the agent of God's
and Christ's activity in the world, and in this way the Spirit
gradually comes to be regarded as a Person because he does the
kind of things a person does. But this again is not completely
clear in Paul, and the Spirit appears in some instances to be a
'thing' which God uses rather than a 'person' who initiates
activity.

5–8. Two possibilities exist for the believer: that his *outlook*
should be *formed* either by his lower nature or by the Spirit; the
second possibility does not exist for unbelievers. The *outlook* of
the *lower nature* is sin and that results in death (cf. 6: 23; 7: 11).
Sin is also *enmity* towards God (cf. 5: 10) since it contravenes his
law and thereby rebels against him. Those who break God's
law do not *please* him. Paul implies that *the outlook of the lower
nature* not only does not *please* God but that it *cannot* do so—
sin can never please God and the *lower nature* is caught by sin
(7: 5, 18). The *spiritual outlook* is not the outlook of a higher
nature in man which thinks good thoughts and performs
religious actions. It is the outlook of the *Spirit* of God which
produces goodness in man (cf. Gal. 5: 22, quoted above), which
makes peace between him and God (5: 1, 10), and gives him
life (5: 21). He would not normally expect to receive any of
these gifts until the coming of the New Age, but by the *Spirit*
they are his now. As we saw above, the *Spirit* was associated
with the Messiah who was expected in the New Age; but for
the Christian the Messiah was Jesus who had already come, so

the Spirit must be active already. We find that at Pentecost, when the first Christians were given the Spirit, Peter in his sermon on that day quoted a passage from the Old Testament which spoke of the coming of the Spirit in the New Age. He went on to argue that this was what had actually happened that very day (Joel 2: 28–9 = Acts 2: 17–18: 'God says, "This will happen in the last days: I will pour out upon everyone a portion of my spirit; and your sons and daughters shall prophesy; your young men shall see visions, and your old men shall dream dreams. Yes, I will endue even my slaves, both men and women, with a portion of my spirit, and they shall prophesy"'; cf. Rom. 8: 23).

9–10. Paul speaks directly to his readers again. They *have been justified* and therefore their 'outlook' is being formed by the Spirit, i.e. they are on the level of the Spirit (once again *spiritual* does not mean 'religious' or represent a higher aspect of man's being, but refers to the Spirit of God). It is indeed impossible to be *Christian* and not possess the *Spirit*, for union with Christ (cf. verse 1) and union with the Spirit go together; either the *Spirit* or *Christ* can be described as *dwelling* in the Christian; the meaning is the same; the real alternative to both is sin dwelling in him (7: 20, where 'lodging' represents the same Greek word as 'dwelling' here); whichever *dwells* in him directs him and forms his outlook. The Christian's *body* is *dead* (in a sense it is really the Christian who is dead, but death is seen in the body and the body is the Christian himself—see on 6:12–13), for he has died with Christ (6: 1–11), this death being required because of his sin. On the other hand God's *Spirit* gives him *life* because he has been *justified* (1: 16–17); because the *Spirit dwells* in him as a justified Christian, *life* is necessarily present.

11. Christians begin now to possess *life* and they will possess it in full when the Old Age has completely passed away and the New Age alone remains. *Jesus* was *raised* by God's *Spirit* into this New Age (cf. 1: 4) and as the Christian is united with Christ so he may expect to be raised like him (6: 5–8). On earth man

(= the *body*; see on verses 9–10 and 6:12–13) is *mortal*, but the *new life* will be eternal (5: 21).

Paul has now finished working out his text in 1: 16–17 and has shown that the righteousness of God leads to life for the man of faith. But he has more to say about the nature of that life. ✻

LIFE IN THE SPIRIT AS SONSHIP

It follows, my friends, that our lower nature has no claim 12 upon us; we are not obliged to live on that level. If you do 13 so, you must die. But if by the Spirit you put to death all the base pursuits of the body, then you will live.

For all who are moved by the Spirit of God are sons of 14 God. The Spirit you have received is not a spirit of slavery 15 leading you back into a life of fear, but a Spirit that makes us sons, enabling us to cry 'Abba! Father!' In that cry the 16 Spirit of God joins with our spirit in testifying that we are God's children; and if children, then heirs. We are God's 17 heirs and Christ's fellow-heirs, if we share his sufferings now in order to share his splendour hereafter.

✻ Because the Christian has entered the life lived on the level of the Spirit, he must seek to live always on that level (verses 12–13). That level is now explained as sonship (verses 14–17): because the Spirit dwells in him he is a son of God and therefore can both call God 'Father' and share as an heir in the inheritance of God.

12–13. Summing up the argument of the preceding section and exhorting them to follow up the new way of life which has been opened up for them by the Spirit's indwelling (8: 9), Paul addresses them more intimately as his *friends*. They are free from the lower nature and the sin and death (cf. pp. 60–1) which result from it (8: 2). If they fall back into that type of life they will still *die*, for death is the punishment for sin. To follow *the base pursuits of the body* would be to live at the level of the lower nature (*body* and 'lower nature' are here the same); they are listed in Gal. 5: 19–20 as 'fornication, impurity, and indecency; idolatry and sorcery; quarrels, a contentious temper, envy, fits of rage, selfish ambitions, dissensions, party intrigues, and jealousies; drinking bouts, orgies, and the like' (cf. Col. 3: 5). It can be seen that these are as much mental and spiritual activities as those which we term bodily. To say, '*Put* these *to death*' is almost the same as saying 'Do not sin', but emphasizes more clearly the effort involved. The presence of the Spirit is not the end of the struggle against sin; it is really the beginning, for only now can it be undertaken successfully. The refusal by means of the help of the Spirit to follow these *base pursuits* results in life (the 'life' of 1: 17; 5: 21; 8: 11). Verses 14–17 explain the nature of that life.

14–15. Those *who are moved by the Spirit of God* to fight the 'base pursuits of the body' (verse 13) are *sons of God*, and they are only able to fight because the Spirit dwells in them (8: 9). Their sonship depends not on the issue of the fight but on the presence of the Spirit, and is therefore a consequence of their justification. It is not suggested here that men are sons of God because he created them, and that the Spirit awakens them to realize this. The *Spirit makes* them *sons*, creating a new relationship for them with God. They are thus set free by the *Spirit* from slavery either to sin (6: 15–19), or to the law (6: 14) which they cannot obey (7:7–25), and which therefore brings *fear* because of their failure to please God. *Fear* is an inevitable part of a religion of law, and it is the kind of *fear* which is terror and anxiety rather than reverence towards God. Since they are sons they can call God their *Father*. *Abba* is a word in Aramaic (the language commonly used in Palestine then) which means *Father*, the word Jesus used when speaking of God. It is the familiar word which a child would use for its own father; the Jews thought it too intimate a word to apply to God; that Jesus used it makes us realize how close he felt to God. Because of its importance for him, the early Christians preserved it. (Other Aramaic words of Jesus are found in Mark 5: 41; 7: 34.) It may be a reference here to the Lord's Prayer which began with it, but more probably it was a whole prayer in itself, a short sharp cry by the Christian under great emotion in which he felt that he was led by the Spirit of God (cf. 8: 26); it was both a prayer to God and a joyful affirmation of what the Christian believed about God.

16. This verse is difficult. It is not clear to whom *the Spirit of God* and *our* human *spirit* jointly testify by their *cry*. The cry is inspired by God's Spirit, otherwise the human *spirit* could never utter it; thus there is really no joint cry in which our human spirit co-operates with God's Spirit. An alternative and equally valid translation would run: 'the Spirit of God testifies to our spirit that we are God's children': this translation is to be preferred. There is no distinction between 'sons' (verse 14) and *children*.

17. Paul uses the image of the children as sharing in what the father bequeaths. God, of course, does not die (the metaphor fails at this point), but the children still inherit. It is an image used in the Old Testament where Israel is said to inherit its land (Gen. 15: 7; 28: 4, etc.). God's true *heir* is 'his own Son' Jesus (8: 3). *Christ* is by his very nature Son of God; Christians are only 'made' so in God's goodness by the Spirit of God. They have no right to the inheritance. But, once made a son, the Christian becomes a *fellow-heir* with Jesus (e.g. he uses the same word 'Father' to address God as Jesus did). The inheritance is the *splendour* of God; much more is said of this in 8: 18–30. *If* means 'since': it does not imply any doubt either that we are *God's heirs* or that we shall *share* in the *splendour hereafter. Suffering* is the lot of every Christian: Jesus said, 'Anyone who wishes to be a follower of mine must leave self behind; he must take up his cross, and come with me' (Mark 8: 34). To suffer with Jesus is not the same as to die with him (6: 3–11). Jesus died, and men are joined to his death through baptism, so that their death is past. But suffering does not belong to the past. Jesus as the head of the new humanity dies as men's representative (5: 12–21; 6: 1–11), but he is not their representative in suffering. Jesus'

earthly life was one of suffering and the lives of his followers are also. Suffering however is not necessarily physical and may be in the mind or heart as much as in the body. This suffering must be distinguished from the trials that impinge on everyone just because they are human beings, e.g. sickness, accident, death of a loved person; rather it is the suffering which comes because Jesus is followed. *

SUFFERING AND THE ASSURANCE OF SPLENDOUR

18 For I reckon that the sufferings we now endure bear no comparison with the splendour, as yet unrevealed, which
19 is in store for us. For the created universe waits with eager
20 expectation for God's sons to be revealed. It was made the victim of frustration, not by its own choice, but because of
21 him who made it so; yet always there was hope, because the universe itself is to be freed from the shackles of mortality and enter upon the liberty and splendour of the chil-
22 dren of God. Up to the present, we know, the whole created universe groans in all its parts as if in the pangs of
23 childbirth. Not only so, but even we, to whom the Spirit is given as firstfruits of the harvest to come, are groaning inwardly while we wait for God to make us his sons and
24 set our whole body free. For we have been saved, though only in hope. Now to see is no longer to hope: why should
25 a man endure and wait for what he already sees? But if we hope for something we do not yet see, then, in waiting for it, we show our endurance.

26   In the same way the Spirit comes to the aid of our weakness. We do not even know how we ought to pray, but through our inarticulate groans the Spirit himself is plead-
27 ing for us, and God who searches our inmost being knows what the Spirit means, because he pleads for God's own

people in God's own way; and in everything, as we know, 28
he co-operates for good with those who love God and are
called according to his purpose. For God knew his own 29
before ever they were, and also ordained that they should
be shaped to the likeness of his Son, that he might be the
eldest among a large family of brothers; and it is these, so 30
fore-ordained, whom he has also called. And those whom
he called he has justified, and to those whom he justified he
has also given his splendour.

✻ Suffering is the lot not only of the Christian but also of the
whole universe. One day, however, there will be a renewed
universe free from suffering; this will come through the deliverance, which is already taking place, of man from sin and
death. Both man and the universe yearn eagerly for its accom-
plishment, and it will certainly take place, because it is part of
God's plan. In the meantime, God by his Spirit helps man in his
weakness.

18. Paul takes up the relationship of *suffering* and *splendour*, to
which he has already drawn attention in verse 17, and makes it
the theme of this section. The mere fact of suffering does not in
itself ensure *splendour*, for Paul refers only to the *sufferings* which
the Christian shares with Christ (verse 17). Viewed against the
background of God's whole purpose these sufferings are not as
fearful as they appear for they *bear no comparison with the splendour* which Christ's followers will enjoy when the Old Age has
completely disappeared and the New Age fully come. Because
of sin the Old Age had been deprived of splendour (3: 23).

19-22. Paul holds here to the Jewish belief that there was a
very close connexion between the fate of man and the fate of
the *created universe*. When Adam fell, his sin affected not only
himself and other men but also the *universe* as a whole, and its
goodness was corrupted: 'And unto Adam he [God] said,
"Because thou hast hearkened unto the voice of thy wife, and
hast eaten of the tree, of which I commanded thee, saying,

'Thou shalt not eat of it'; cursed is the ground for thy sake"'
(Gen. 3: 17). Because of man's sin God *made* the universe *the
victim of frustration*; much of the suffering that comes through
the universe (natural disasters, as distinct from the sufferings of
Christians in verses 17–18) seems without purpose. But God
also gave *hope* to the universe: if man is saved, then through
him the universe itself might be saved. As man was freed from
death, the punishment for sin, so the universe would be *freed from
the shackles of mortality*, i.e. from its own purposeless destructive-
ness. Thus the universe is said to wait *with eager expectation
for God's sons to be revealed*. In the present period when the Old
and the New Age exist simultaneously, the fact that Christians
are *God's sons* is not apparent; but when the New Age is fully
come then they will *be revealed* to all creation as such, and as the
new humanity they will exercise a new lordship over creation.

Originally God had given man such a lordship: 'And God
said [to the man and woman whom he had made], "Behold, I
have given you every herb yielding seed ... and every tree ...
and every beast of the earth..."' (Gen. 1: 29–30); cf. 'Thou
madest him [man] to have dominion over the works of thy
hands' (Ps. 8: 6). But man sinned and misruled the universe;
many natural disasters are the fault of his misuse of his power
over nature, e.g. large areas of fertile country in North America
and Africa have been overcropped and as a result become in-
fertile (the 'dust-bowl'). The new humanity would bring creation back to what the biblical writers conceived as its original
state of perfection: 'God saw everything that he had made, and,
behold, it was very good' (Gen. 1: 31). Thus the Bible looks to
a reconstituted and perfect universe—a new heaven and a new
earth (Isa. 66: 22; Rev. 21: 1). Then the *created universe* would
enjoy the *liberty and splendour of the children of God* (verse 21). At
present this belongs to the future and so the universe *groans*.

the pangs of childbirth (verse 22) was a common Jewish metaphor for the suffering that would precede the coming of the
new Age: e.g. Isa. 26: 17 (a passage in which the imminence of
the New Age is strongly felt), 'Like as a woman with child, that

98

draweth near the time of her delivery, is in pain and crieth out in her pangs: so have we been before thee, O Lord.'

Paul's thought is difficult for us, because while we can understand that some natural disasters are due to man and would not occur if man were perfect, others, e.g. earthquakes, seem to have nothing to do with his folly and were in the world before he ever appeared; there was no originally good world which became corrupted. But we can appreciate the point that a new universe and a new humanity go together: a perfect universe requires perfect men that it may remain perfect, and perfect men require a perfect universe in which to exercise their perfection. The fate of the universe depends on man, and his fate depends on that of Jesus in the cross and resurrection (5: 12–21; 6: 1–11).

23–5. Even more than 'the created universe' (verses 19–22) Christians who have received the Spirit *are groaning inwardly*. *firstfruits* were the first part of the harvest to be gathered; they were dedicated to God (Lev. 23: 15–21). The feast at which this was offered later came to be known as Pentecost, and it was at its celebration that the *Spirit* was first *given* to the Church (Acts 2: 1–4). Christians thus have the *Spirit, the firstfruits of the harvest*, but *groan inwardly* for the fullness of the harvest. Some early manuscripts omit the words *make us his sons and* (verse 23) which appear to contradict 8: 15. If they are retained, the idea is that though Christians are already sons they have not yet entered into their inheritance (8: 17), and they will do this only when the *harvest* is fully come. Paul does not say in what the fullness of the *harvest* consists; it means at least that the *body* will be *set free*. The Christian is not to be *set free* from his *body*, but his *body* (i.e. himself) is to be *set free* from 'mortality' (verse 21; cf. 7: 24 and I Cor. 15: 53, 'What is mortal must be clothed with immortality'). This still belongs to the future and is therefore a matter of *hope* (verse 24): if it were already present we would *see* it. Our *salvation* is certain: in *hope* (a hope which is placed in God and not in ourselves) it is already ours and therefore we can *wait* and *endure* our present sufferings (verse 18).

26–7. The Christian has received the *Spirit* (verse 23) and the

99

Spirit assists him where he is weak. We have already seen that he is weak to do God's will (7: 14–25); this *weakness* includes not only his words and actions but even his inward life in his prayers. This does not mean merely that he does not know perfectly the technique of prayer (such things as how far he should use written prayers, or how he should control his mind from wandering), but that even his best prayers are not prayed *in God's own way*. There is always too much of himself in his prayers; he prays for the wrong things; he does not really want what God wants. When we realize the inability of our prayers to please God, then through *our inarticulate groans* (cf. verses 22–3) the *Spirit...pleads for* us. The second *our* in verse 26 is not in the Greek and the *groans* may be those of the Spirit; indeed even our groans become his when he pleads through them. The conception here of the *Spirit* who *pleads* is similar to what we find in John's Gospel, where the Spirit is called our 'advocate' (14: 16, 26; 15: 26; 16: 7). And when he *pleads for* us God who knows our *inmost being knows* even more *what the Spirit means*, for he talks God's language. Thus our hopelessly inadequate prayers become real prayers.

28. *as we know*: Paul introduces teaching already known to his readers which he adapts to his own purpose; for the assurance that the Christian will receive the 'splendour, as yet unrevealed', but 'in store for' him (verse 18) rests, not on the Christian's own faith or actions, but on what God has done (verses 29–30). *In everything*, including his suffering and his prayers (verses 18–27), the Spirit *co-operates* with the Christian, i.e. the one *who loves God*, for his final *good* and salvation. A possible misunderstanding must be removed: it is not because a man loves God that the Spirit co-operates with him; *those who love God* are at once redefined as those who *are called according to his* [God's] *purpose*. Men can really only *love God* in so far as God helps them to do it, even as they can only pray in so far as the Spirit helps them (verse 26); God, however, will help them because he has included their love in his *purpose* or plan. We should note that there are two other possible renderings of this

verse: God may be taken as the subject of *co-operates* and this does not change the meaning very much; or it may be rendered 'everything co-operates for good...' This latter translation is implied by many manuscripts; it should not be taken to teach that everything will always work for the best for men; since God's *purpose* governs all to which this verse applies, it is only as he plans that *everything* can work for men's good.

29–30. *God knew* them: not just in the sense of knowing what would happen to them or of knowing who they were but rather as one person knows another as a friend. The word 'know' is used here by Paul in the way it is often used in the Old Testament, e.g. Amos 3: 2, 'You only have I known of all the families of the earth', where it means that God 'chose and cared' for the Israelites. Since *God knew* them in this way he planned that *they should be shaped to the likeness of his Son*. Jesus is the *likeness* or 'very image' of God (2 Cor. 4: 4; cf. Col. 1: 15). Man was originally made in God's 'image' and 'likeness' (Gen. 1: 26) but lost that likeness, as he also lost the 'splendour' (3: 23), by his sin. As a member of the new humanity in the fully restored New Age, he will regain both the *likeness* and the *splendour* which Jesus already possesses. This does not mean that the Christian will be the same as Jesus: the latter will retain his unique position as being the *eldest among a large family of brothers* (cf. 8: 17), and the Christian only receives the *likeness* and *splendour* through Jesus. Verse 29 speaks of God's purpose and intention; verse 30 tells how it is achieved: men are *called* by God through preaching (10: 14–15); they respond in faith and are *justified*, and so are given God's *splendour*. Paul writes as if they already possessed the *splendour*. They do, in so far as they already belong to the New Age; but in so far as they continue to live in the Old Age, as they must while they are on earth, it is a *splendour* 'as yet unrevealed' (8: 18).

The conception of God's plan and purpose is taken up again in chapters 9–11 and we shall deal there with some of the difficulties centring on the word *fore-ordained* which it appears to raise. ✳

VICTORY THROUGH GOD'S LOVE

31 With all this in mind, what are we to say? If God is on our
32 side, who is against us? He did not spare his own Son, but
surrendered him for us all; and with this gift how can he
33 fail to lavish upon us all he has to give? Who will be the
accuser of God's chosen ones? It is God who pronounces
34 acquittal: then who can condemn? It is Christ—Christ who
died, and, more than that, was raised from the dead—who
35 is at God's right hand, and indeed pleads our cause. Then
what can separate us from the love of Christ? Can affliction
or hardship? Can persecution, hunger, nakedness, peril, or
36 the sword? 'We are being done to death for thy sake all day
long,' as Scripture says; 'we have been treated like sheep
37 for slaughter'—and yet, in spite of all, overwhelming vic-
38 tory is ours through him who loved us. For I am convinced that there is nothing in death or life, in the realm of
spirits or superhuman powers, in the world as it is or the
39 world as it shall be, in the forces of the universe, in heights
or depths—nothing in all creation that can separate us
from the love of God in Christ Jesus our Lord.

⁎ Because of what God has done in the death and resurrection
of Jesus, the believer has nothing to fear either in the present
condition of the world from evil men and evil spiritual forces,
or in the world to come when God judges men. His security
rests on God's love made known in Jesus. In their language and
rhythm these verses sound like a hymn.

31–2. Recalling to his readers all that he has said of what God
has done on their behalf (e.g. 8: 1, 29–30), Paul draws the irre-
sistible conclusion: *If God is on our side, who is against us?* The
picture is that of a court of law in which God, who is the judge,
is also the advocate appearing for us. No advocate *against us* can
possibly triumph over him. And because God is on our side,

there is nothing which he will not give us; of this our guarantee is the fact that he has already given *his own Son*. As Abraham *did not spare his own son*, Isaac, but was ready to sacrifice him at God's command (though he did not in the end have to carry out the sacrifice—see Gen. 22), so God *did not spare* Jesus. God not only makes *this gift* to us, but with it he justifies us, 'makes us sons' and 'Christ's fellow-heirs' (8: 15–17) and gives us life (1: 17; 8: 6, 11).

33–4. No man on earth, nor angel in heaven, nor even the devil will dare to accuse us before God because he 'is on our side' (verse 31), and we are those whom he has *chosen* for himself. There is no judge other than God and, since we already know that he has pronounced *acquittal* over us (8: 1), there is no one who can *condemn* us in the day of judgement. Moreover we have another advocate who *pleads our cause*, the Son whom God gave for us and who *died;* even now he is present with God to plead for us who are his 'fellow-heirs' and who 'share his sufferings now' (8: 17). The *right hand* was the traditional place of honour beside a king, giving the occupant direct access to him.

35–7. Christ loved us in his death and now pleads for us (verse 34), and because he loves us nothing can separate us from him. The trials instanced by Paul are the kind of thing he himself experienced in his journeying as a Christian missionary (see the long list in 2 Cor. 11: 23–7); in 1 Cor. 15: 31 he says, 'every day I die', showing the constant peril in which he and his readers stood. There had been no general persecution of Christians by the Roman authorities at the time he wrote; but a zealous minority, like the Christian community, always attracts unfavourable attention and would therefore suffer from mob violence and occasional official action (cf. pp. 149–50). Verse 36, a quotation from Ps. 44: 22, declares that as Jesus' *death* was in accordance with Scripture, so also are the sufferings of Christians. God does not remove such trials from our path; they are overcome in an *overwhelming victory* because we have 'strength for anything through him (i.e. Jesus) who gives' us 'power' (Phil. 4: 13), and 'the Spirit comes to the aid of our weakness' (8: 26).

38–9. Finally in a word of personal testimony, based not on his personal experience of every trial but on his certainty of God's love, Paul affirms that there is *nothing* whatsoever *that can separate us from the love of God in Christ Jesus our Lord: nothing in death* (which brings God's judgement (verses 31–4)) *or life* (which brings the trials inflicted by men (verses 35–7))—thus he sums up the previous verses. And the same certainty is true of other areas: the men of that time believed the world was controlled by evil *spirits* and *superhuman powers*; often associated with planets (*heights, depths* are astrological terms). These determined their destiny from birth to death and beyond death, in the present condition of the world and in 'the pangs of childbirth' (8: 22) by which the New Age will come into full existence (*the world as it is or shall be*); they were thought responsible for every kind of natural disaster which might destroy life (*the forces of the universe*). Paul neither says nor denies that these evil forces exist, but he affirms that if they do they are utterly incapable of frustrating God's purpose of love towards those whom he has called and justified (8: 30).

This brings us to the end of the third main section (chapters 5–8). Having shown that all men need to be put right with God (1: 18 — 3: 20) and that God has taken action to put them right with himself (3: 21 — 4: 25), Paul has now made it clear that to be put right with God is not a mere sentence of acquittal, leaving a man in the same position as he was before he heard it except that he has been declared innocent. Instead, he has thereby been brought into a new situation: he has entered a new life, become the member of a new humanity whose head and first member is Jesus; he has been given the assistance of God's Spirit in his own weakness and he is assured that God in his love will preserve him and bring him to enjoy the splendour that belongs to the children of God (5: 1 — 8: 39).

Paul has now prepared a position from which he can appeal to the Christian to show righteousness in his daily life (12: 1 ff.), but before turning to that he discusses the place of Jews and Gentiles in God's plan (9: 1 — 11: 36). ✳

The Purpose of God in History

❋ Paul has a difficult problem on his hands. In his argument he has quoted the Old Testament again and again; in particular he has grounded his teaching about justification by faith in Old Testament promises (e.g. 1: 17; 4: 3). If these promises stand, must not those promises also stand which affirm that the Jews are God's people? Paul has continually drawn attention to the new humanity which has come into being through Christ; the majority of its members are Gentiles and not Jews, and many Jews oppose it as once they opposed and rejected Jesus. How then can it be God's people? God definitely 'called' the Jews, but they would appear to have been deprived, or to have deprived themselves, of 'his splendour' (8: 30). Is there no place left for them in the way God works out history? Can their 'faithlessness cancel' God's plans (cf. 3: 3-4)? This may not seem a very real problem for those who have no actual contact with Jews and for whom they seem another race and religion. It was, however, a serious problem for the early Christians, the first of whom had all been Jews, like Paul, or though born as Gentiles made continual use of the sacred writings of the Jews and believed their faith went back to Abraham (chapter 4). It still is a problem for all who realize how much Christianity and Judaism have in common. To answer it, Paul shows that even though the majority of Jews rejected Jesus, the promises made to them are not null and void but continue to be valid. Thus, though at first sight he appears to be entering in chapters 9-11 on an entirely new and rather remote subject, this is not so. ❋

GRIEF AND SORROW OVER ISRAEL

I AM SPEAKING the truth as a Christian, and my own **9**
conscience, enlightened by the Holy Spirit, assures me
it is no lie: in my heart there is great grief and unceasing 2

3 sorrow. For I could even pray to be outcast from Christ myself for the sake of my brothers, my natural kinsfolk.
4 They are Israelites: they were made God's sons; theirs is the splendour of the divine presence, theirs the covenants, the law, the temple worship, and the promises.
5 Theirs are the patriarchs, and from them, in natural descent, sprang the Messiah. May God, supreme above all, be blessed for ever! Amen.

* In a matter of deep importance to himself and the Christian church, namely the failure of the Jews to accept Jesus as their Messiah, Paul begins by solemnly affirming that he speaks the truth. His sorrow is so profound that he would gladly suffer damnation if he thought that in any way it would bring salvation to the Jews who had enjoyed every privilege from God.

1–2. Since Paul had concentrated so much of his preaching on the Gentiles, it might have been thought that he was a traitor to his own people or that he did not care what happened to them. The very opposite is true: *great grief and unceasing sorrow* grip him because of their unbelief.

3. Paul could conceive of no worse fate than *to be outcast from Christ*; it would have meant losing all the privileges and joys of Christian life and coming under the judgement of God. Yet he would be willing to suffer this—supposing it were possible (cf. 8: 38–9)—if it brought the Jews to accept Jesus. Once, earlier, when Israel had sinned, Moses prayed for God to forgive them, 'and if not, blot me, I pray thee, out of thy book which thou hast written' (Exod. 32: 32). Moses is willing to disappear, along with his people, out of God's plans; Paul, however, is willing to be rejected in order that his own nation may not be rejected. Here is a depth of love which can only have been awakened in Paul by the realization that God loved him (5: 6–8).

4–5. Paul lists the privileges that the Jews enjoyed as God's people.

Israelites: Israel was the special name given to Jacob by God and meant first of all Jacob himself and then all his descendants; it implied that they all had a unique place in God's plans.

splendour of the divine presence: God was believed to have been present with the Jews as they journeyed out of Egypt to the Promised Land and to be present in the temple at Jerusalem.

covenants: the agreements that God made with Abraham, Isaac and Jacob, and then with Israel as a whole at the Exodus, that he was their God and they were his people and that therefore they should serve him.

promises: the prophecies of the Old Testament, in particular those relating to the Messiah.

patriarchs: Abraham, Isaac, Jacob, and his twelve sons, and the other great men of Israel's past.

The last sentence of verse 5 is difficult. The N.E.B. gives in its footnote two other ways of taking the words: either (*a*) '...sprang the Messiah, supreme above all, God blessed for ever!' or (*b*) '...sprang the Messiah, who is supreme above all. Blessed be God for ever!'

These differences arise because ancient manuscripts were not punctuated. Normally it is easy to guess the punctuation to be inserted, but there are one or two places, as here, where this is difficult and the choice of punctuation affects the sense. The first alternative is the most natural way of taking the Greek, but it is argued against it that Paul nowhere else terms Jesus 'God'. However it does not imply that Jesus is to be identified with God, but only that he is divine, and this is not at variance with other statements Paul makes about him. Moreover it balances a statement about the human side of Jesus (*natural descent*) with one about his divine side as in 1: 3–4, and gives a truly fitting climax to the list of the privileges which Israel has had—the divine *Messiah*. If we take the verse as in the N.E.B. text, then it is a typical 'blessing of God'; such blessings are found in Jewish (and later in Christian) writings as a response to the recollection of God's goodness. ✳

GOD'S SELECTIVE PURPOSE

6 It is impossible that the word of God should have proved
7 false. For not all descendants of Israel are truly Israel, nor,
because they are Abraham's offspring, are they all his true
children; but, in the words of Scripture, 'Through the line
8 of Isaac your posterity shall be traced.' That is to say, it is
not those born in the course of nature who are children of
God; it is the children born through God's promise who
9 are reckoned as Abraham's descendants. For the promise
runs: 'At the time fixed I will come, and Sarah shall have a
son.'

10 But that is not all, for Rebekah's children had one and
11 the same father, our ancestor Isaac; and yet, in order that
God's selective purpose might stand, based not upon men's
12 deeds but upon the call of God, she was told, even before
they were born, when they had as yet done nothing, good
13 or ill, 'The elder shall be servant to the younger'; and that
accords with the text of Scripture, 'Jacob I loved and Esau I
hated.'

* God has made his promises to Israel, and since they are God's
promises they cannot possibly fail; yet the people of Israel
appear to have rejected their supreme privilege, the Messiah.
How can this be? Paul answers the difficulty by explaining what
the name Israel really means: it is not identical with the descendants of Abraham, as the history of Israel shows. God had always
been free in the past to select those who would constitute
Israel, and therefore still is.

6. *the word of God* which cannot prove *false* is that the privileges listed in verses 4–5 and given by God to Israel must still belong to Israel.

7. *Israel* is now redefined. Though Abraham had several

sons, only two are important here for Paul's thought, Ishmael and *Isaac*. Ishmael, the older, was the son of Hagar who was the servant of Sarah, the wife of Abraham (Gen. 16). According to the customs of the time he might have been expected to be included in *Israel* if it consisted of the *descendants* of *Abraham*. But God selected only the second-born son *Isaac*, whose mother was Sarah, and *Israel* was therefore continued through *Isaac* alone. The quotation is from Gen. 21: 12.

8–9. Isaac was born when his parents were long past the normal age for having children (4: 19–20) as the result of a special *promise* of God (Gen. 18: 10, quoted in verse 9). Years earlier, when it seemed that he would have no children by *Sarah*, Ishmael had been Abraham's own attempt to ensure for himself *descendants* to whom 'the word of God' (verse 6) would apply. Since God provided Isaac, it was only to be expected that he and his *descendants* should constitute Israel.

10–13. But not even all of *Isaac's* descendants are reckoned within Israel. Paul realizes that his opponents might object that Ishmael was not Sarah's son, and so he shows how in the case of Isaac's twin sons *Esau* and *Jacob* only one was chosen, and that one was Jacob, the younger. The choice indeed was made *even before they were born*. Membership in Israel is not a matter of *men's* good *deeds*. What Paul says here is obviously in keeping with what he wrote earlier about justification: men are justified not through what they have done (3: 20, 28), but by 'God's free grace alone' (3: 24). So membership in Israel does not depend on birth nor on success in life but on *God's selective purpose* (verse 11). These last words are the key phrase in the passage: God is free to choose to whom his promises apply. It is the unspoken conclusion at this point that if God was once free to choose among the descendants of Abraham so he is now free to choose outside their number; and in chapter 11 Paul stresses that this is what God has done. God's promises apply, not to those who can trace their physical descent to Abraham, but to those who have faith like Abraham (chapter 4). The theoretical background to God's choice was already given in 8: 28–30.

12–13. The two quotations in verses 12 and 13 come from Gen. 25: 23 and Mal. 1: 2–3 respectively. When we examine them in their context we see that they do not apply to the two individuals *Jacob* and *Esau* but to the two peoples, the Jews and the Edomites, who are descended from them; this is how Paul uses the words here. In this passage Paul is not writing about God's choice of particular persons, to save some and to reject others, but of his choice of the Jews, rejecting the Edomites, to use them in his plan to save men. There is no suggestion that God chose Jacob because he foresaw the kind of person Esau turned out to be.

The words *love* and *hate* are strong. They should not be understood as if God acted in an emotional way. His love for *Jacob* means that he applied his promises to the Jews, and his hatred for *Esau* that he disregarded the Edomites. He acts in this way, not for the good of Jacob nor to injure Esau, but in order to carry out his plans. It does not mean that *Jacob* is automatically saved and *Esau* rejected. ✻

GOD'S FREEDOM TO CHOOSE

14 What shall we say to that? Is God to be charged with in-
15 justice? By no means. For he says to Moses, 'Where I show mercy, I will show mercy, and where I pity, I will pity.'
16 Thus it does not depend on man's will or effort, but on
17 God's mercy. For Scripture says to Pharaoh, 'I have raised you up for this very purpose, to exhibit my power in my dealings with you, and to spread my fame over all the
18 world.' Thus he not only shows mercy as he chooses, but also makes men stubborn as he chooses.

19   You will say, 'Then why does God blame a man? For
20 who can resist his will?' Who are you, sir, to answer God back? Can the pot speak to the potter and say, 'Why did
21 you make me like this?' Surely the potter can do what he

likes with the clay. Is he not free to make out of the same lump two vessels, one to be treasured, the other for common use?

But what if God, desiring to exhibit his retribution at 22 work and to make his power known, tolerated very patiently those vessels which were objects of retribution due for destruction, and did so in order to make known the 23 full wealth of his splendour upon vessels which were objects of mercy, and which from the first had been prepared for this splendour?

Such vessels are we, whom he has called from among 24 Gentiles as well as Jews, as it says in the Book of Hosea: 25 'Those who were not my people I will call My People, and the unloved nation I will call My Beloved. For in the very 26 place where they were told "you are no people of mine", they shall be called Sons of the living God.' But Isaiah 27 makes this proclamation about Israel: 'Though the Israelites be countless as the sands of the sea, it is but a remnant that shall be saved; for the Lord's sentence on the land will 28 be summary and final'; as also he said previously, 'If the 29 Lord of Hosts had not left us the mere germ of a nation, we should have become like Sodom, and no better than Gomorrah.'

* Paul continues his argument that God is free to choose whom he wishes to include in his people, and that in so doing he chooses from the Gentiles as well as the Jews. This freedom on God's part belongs to his very nature as God and neither means that he acts unfairly (verses 14–18) nor that he wrongly blames men for what they have been chosen by him to do (verses 19–21). Whatever he does, he does it to have mercy on men, even though it means he uses those whom it would appear he

ought to punish; it is all part of his plan to bring salvation. Paul supports his argument with quotations from the Old Testament which ought to strike home with Jewish Christian readers.

14. Paul imagines an objection raised. If God loved Jacob and hated Esau before either was born, would he not have been acting unjustly? Throughout the letter Paul has been discussing 'God's justice' or righteousness and therefore he must deal with this criticism.

15-16. He answers it with another Old Testament quotation (from Exod. 33: 19) which he generalizes into the statement of verse 16. What he says is in keeping with his earlier argument that what man does is useless to earn favour with God (3 : 9-20). If God were to act on the strict principle that he *showed mercy* only to those who had earned it, it would not be *mercy* (see the discussion on 4: 3-5).

17-18. The question becomes more acute when God appears deliberately to refuse mercy to some, and Paul now instances *Pharaoh*, the ruler of Egypt, who at the time of the Exodus had striven to retain the Israelites as slaves in Egypt. Paul, quoting Exod. 9: 16, argues that this had been part of the plan of God, who *makes men stubborn as he chooses*.

Paul is not writing here about the ultimate personal fate of either Moses or Pharaoh—whether they are saved or not—but about the *purpose* by whose execution God has been able to bring to light his justice (3 : 21) and to right wrong (1 : 17). The very opposition of Pharaoh enabled God to *exhibit* his *power*, and his *fame* was *spread . . . over all the world*. Paul's underlying argument at this point is that the Jews by their *stubborn* rejection of Jesus have actually furthered God's *purpose* to save men, and therefore their opposition is not surprising despite the privileges listed in 9: 4-5.

The idea that God should deliberately make someone *stubborn* is hard to understand. We need to realize that in the Old Testament it says both that God made Pharaoh *stubborn* and also that he (Pharaoh) made himself *stubborn* (Exod. 8: 15). In chapter 10 Paul will go on to argue that Israel also was actually guilty 'because it failed to recognize the message' (10: 19). We have already seen (1: 18–32) how man's rejection of God draws God's retribution on him, and how this in turn drives man more deeply into sin. The relationship between God's creation of man and man's responsibility for his sin is not simple. Paul is very much aware that what he is saying here in chapter 9 might lead to the accusation that he is taking from man his responsibility to act morally (see further, pp. 134–7).

19–21. It is with this objection that he now deals. If God is God, the objector argues, then *his will* is bound to prevail; why then should Pharaoh be *blamed* if he is stubborn (and in the Old Testament God does blame him: Exod. 10: 3, where God says to him, 'How long wilt thou refuse to humble thyself before me?'). In reply Paul uses a common Old Testament metaphor —that of the potter (see e.g. Isa. 29: 16; 45: 9)—and applies it to God's work in moulding the events of history. As the potter can make either a *treasured* vase or a *common* jug, God can make either a Moses responsive to himself or a Pharaoh who will be 'stubborn'. To deny this is really to deny that God is in control of what he makes; he has the right to make men as he wishes. But this does not wholly answer the objection. A man, unlike *clay* made into a *vessel*, can be *blamed* for the function he fulfils, and a Pharaoh may complain that he should not be held to account for stubbornness if he has been made stubborn (verse 18). We should note: (*a*) Paul never denies a man's responsibility for what he does; see note on verses 17–18; (*b*) like the potter who never creates aimlessly—for he has to sell what he makes—God had a purpose when he created a stubborn Pharaoh or an Israel which would reject its Messiah; to this purpose Paul now passes (verses 22–4).

22–3. And God's purpose is that there should be *vessels* (i.e. men) who respond to his *mercy*, and that these should come from among both the Jews and the Gentiles. To achieve this ultimate purpose God endured *those vessels* (i.e. men) who *were objects of retribution due for destruction*. The potter destroys *vessels* that do not come up to his standards; God *tolerates* them.

(We may note in this passage how often the word *mercy* occurs; this ultimately is the main spring of God's activity.) So God tolerated the Jews though they were 'stubborn' (verse 18) vessels and deserved punishment because they continually rebelled against him (as told throughout the Old Testament). He *tolerated* them because eventually 'from them, in natural descent, sprang the Messiah' (9: 5) and through their very rejection of the Messiah his plan of salvation was carried out. God's *retribution* (anger) and *power* are now *exhibited* in the fact that 'not all the descendants of Israel are truly Israel' (9: 7).

24. And now Paul draws his conclusion: there are both *Jews* and *Gentiles* in God's people. Paul began the passage by showing that in actual fact God never did include all the descendants of Abraham and Isaac in Israel; he went on to show that God is free to choose whomever he wishes—consequently he *has called* men from *among Gentiles* and excluded *Jews* who have rejected their Messiah.

25-9. This conclusion is supported by a series of Old Testament quotations. Verses 25 and 26 are separate quotations from Hos. 2: 23 and 1: 10 respectively, verses 27–8 from Isa. 10: 22–3, and verse 29 from Isa. 1: 9. The Jews' own book, the Old Testament, is thus made to show that God would draw into his *People* others as well as the descendants of Abraham. Verses 25-6 refer to a time when the Jewish Kingdom was split and one part had lapsed into virtual paganism; the passage therefore originally applied to Israel itself (see pp. 52–3); but if God could *call* them back to be his *People* then he could equally have mercy on those outside Israel and *call* them. *Call* is used here in the same sense as in 8: 28–30 and means much more than 'name'.

27-9. These quotations both take us back to 9: 6–13 and prepare us for chapter 11. In 9: 6–13 we saw that God selected from among the descendants of Abraham; as the two quotations from Isaiah (10: 22–3 and 1: 9) show, the Old Testament itself recognized that the process of selection continued throughout the history of Israel; at any given time there were only some

Jews who were faithful to God; these are the *remnant that shall be saved*. Israel for her faults deserved to be destroyed as were *Sodom* and *Gomorrah* with brimstone and fire because of their sins (Gen. chapters 18, 19); their sins and their punishment were frequently used as a warning in Jewish literature. God however has 'tolerated' Israel and so his people now includes both Jews and Gentiles.

Earlier Paul had shown that the only true attitude to God is faith, and that whoever has faith, whether Jew or Gentile, is a member of God's people (3: 20 — 4: 25); now he has approached this from another angle and shown that God, as a creator and ruler who always acts in mercy, is free to include both Jews and Gentiles, and has in fact done so; moreover, he has deduced this from the Old Testament itself. ✻

WHY ISRAEL FAILED

Then what are we to say? That Gentiles, who made no 30 effort after righteousness, nevertheless achieved it, a righteousness based on faith; whereas Israel made great 31 efforts after a law of righteousness, but never attained to it. Why was this? Because their efforts were not based on 32 faith, but (as they supposed) on deeds. They stumbled over the 'stumbling-stone' mentioned in Scripture: 'Here I lay 33 in Zion a stumbling-stone and a rock to trip them up; but he who has faith in him will not be put to shame.'

✻ Having shown that God was free to choose whomever he wished to be members of his people (9: 6–29), Paul now begins to show why in actual fact the Jews had failed to accept Jesus as their Messiah and why therefore they were rejected by God. He continues with this theme throughout chapter 10.

30–1. Paul reaffirms the conclusion of 9: 24, one which would have been most surprising to a Jew, and begins to explain it. He has already demonstrated in 3: 21 — 4: 25 that the only *righteousness* which is acceptable to God is that which he himself gives and which is *based on faith*. The Gentiles appear to make *no* great *effort* to be righteous (remember how he characterized the Gentile world in 1: 18–32) and yet some of them have been justified through *faith*. The Jews on the other hand possessed the *law* which might have made them righteous; they made great efforts to live up to it but failed (remember how Paul showed their failure in 2: 1 — 3: 20), and so did not become righteous. Thus what has actually happened accords with the theory Paul has put forward in 9: 6–29.

32. The Jews failed because their *efforts* were *efforts*, i.e. attempts *based on deeds* to win God's favour. *Faith*, or trust, can only operate where *effort* has ceased. When we insist on relying on our own unaided efforts no one can help us, and so we have no opportunity for *faith* in another person.

32–3. The *stumbling-stone* is Jesus for, as Paul has shown in 3: 21–6, he is the means by which God has demonstrated to us his way of 'righteousness based on faith' (verse 30). Because of Jesus' death God's way is one not of 'effort' but of 'faith'. In their 'efforts' to reach righteousness the Jews thus *trip* over him as one might *trip* over a big stone when running a race. But the stone which trips them up is the very stone by which those who have *faith* are saved. The quotation comes from Isa. 28: 16 combined with Isa. 8: 14 and is nearer in wording to the Septuagint than to the Hebrew. The idea of Jesus as a stone of stumbling is common in the New Testament; see Mark 12: 10–11; Acts 4: 11; 1 Pet. 2: 6–8. ✳

TWO KINDS OF RIGHTEOUSNESS

10 Brothers, my deepest desire and my prayer to God is for
2 their salvation. To their zeal for God I can testify; but it is
3 an ill-informed zeal. For they ignore God's way of righteousness, and try to set up their own, and therefore they
have not submitted themselves to God's righteousness.

For Christ ends the law and brings righteousness for every- 4
one who has faith.

Of legal righteousness Moses writes, 'The man who does 5
this shall gain life by it.' But the righteousness that comes 6
by faith says, 'Do not say to yourself, "Who can go up to
heaven?" ' (that is to bring Christ down), 'or, "Who can 7
go down to the abyss?" ' (to bring Christ up from the
dead). But what does it say? 'The word is near you: it is 8
upon your lips and in your heart.' This means the word of
faith which we proclaim. If on your lips is the confession, 9
'Jesus is Lord', and in your heart the faith that God raised
him from the dead, then you will find salvation. For the 10
faith that leads to righteousness is in the heart, and the confession that leads to salvation is upon the lips.

Scripture says, 'Everyone who has faith in him will be 11
saved from shame'—everyone: there is no distinction be- 12
tween Jew and Greek, because the same Lord is Lord of all,
and is rich enough for the need of all who invoke him. For 13
everyone, as it says again—'everyone who invokes the
name of the Lord will be saved'.

✻ Continuing with the discussion of Israel's failure, the contrast between the two types of righteousness indicated in
9: 30–1 is now further explained; Paul lays most of his emphasis on the righteousness which is connected with faith, for he
wishes to show that it is in accord with the Old Testament and
that therefore the Jews are the more at fault if they reject it.

1. The failure of the Jews was both part of God's plan (9:
6–29) and also a matter of their own choice (9: 30–3). Paul cannot be happy with the conclusion that they are outside God's
people, nor can he believe that any exclusion therefrom is final.
If it does not lie within his power to be an 'outcast' (9: 3) for
them, he can at least *pray* that they may be saved. If he seriously

believed that they were irrevocably destined to damnation he would hardly have so prayed.

2-3. Before Paul became a Christian he had shared in the *zeal* of the Jews for God and had persecuted the Christians (see pp. 1 f.). His, like theirs, had been a true zeal, but a misdirected one. They misunderstood how God would save men (*God's way of righteousness* is the same phrase as 'God's way of righting wrong' in 1: 17; see the notes there for its meaning). They knew that *righteousness* was necessary if men were to be accepted by God and they wrongly tried *to set up their own* by their good behaviour. They did not receive obediently (*they have not submitted to*) the *righteousness*, or acquittal and life, that God was ready to give, so that they might be made righteous.

4. They had not realized that with the death of Christ the New Age had come in which obedience to the *law* as a way of being accepted by God was ended. It is replaced by the new way in which God rights wrong (1: 17) for those who have faith and counts them righteous (4: 3). Christ *brings* this righteousness to them; they do not have to labour for it. Two attitudes on man's part are strongly contrasted in verses 2-4: the attempt to keep a law or standard of behaviour as a means to win God's favour, and the acceptance through faith of God's favour because of what God has done by the death and resurrection of Christ (3: 24-6). The second attitude is possible only because God loves men (5: 6-8). In verses 5-13 Paul explores this contrast further.

5. For Paul, *Moses* was the author of the Pentateuch and in effect, therefore, of the law; he quotes him (from Lev. 18: 5) as saying that the man who keeps the law gains *life* (1: 17 showed that it was Paul's aim that men should have *life*). Paul does not contradict Moses; he has however already shown that since all men sin no one will *gain life by* obedience to the law, and has argued that Christ's coming has put an end (10: 4) to this way of gaining life.

6-8. Now Paul goes on to quote from the Law itself (cf. note on 3: 21) further statements which imply that there is another way to righteousness. *Do not say to yourself* comes from Deut. 9: 4, which goes on to remind the Jews that they are not to say with regard to their homeland, 'For my righteousness the Lord hath brought me in to possess this land'. The Promised Land was as much the gift of God's righteousness then as is his gift of Jesus now. Thus the Law itself confirms the *righteousness that comes by faith*.

The remainder of the quotation is from Deut. 30: 11–14. There it applies to the law which is neither far away in *heaven* (i.e. where God lives) nor far away in the abyss (i.e. where the dead live) but *near* (i.e. with the Israelites) because God has given it to them. At first sight it seems strange that Paul takes this passage, which refers to the law, and applies it to Jesus and the *righteousness* through *faith*. He does so because: (i) the law is regarded as God's gift, just as Jesus is; (ii) *word*, which comes in the quotation, was one of the terms used by the early Christians to denote the Gospel, and Paul understands it in that way here; (iii) Jesus ended the law (10: 4), not only in the way we have explained there but also in the sense that he kept it perfectly, or fulfilled it; therefore he has now taken its place and a text referring to it may be applied to him; (iv) the passage fits Jesus' case exactly: the Jews do not now need to *go up to heaven* to call down their Messiah; in the birth of Jesus he came down and is *near;* nor do the Jews need to go down to the place of the dead to fetch him; he has already risen from the dead. It is impossible to produce Christ; not even perfect obedience will do it; for he is already here. Thus the Jews have no excuse, because *the righteousness that comes by faith* is not remote from them but with them through the Christians who *proclaim* it; it is the *word* or message which challenges men to *faith*.

9–10. Put very briefly, this 'word' is '*Jesus is Lord*'. This affirmation was used in the early church as a public avowal of faith. If a man was prepared to say this he would be recognized as a member of the church and baptized. Words and thought cannot however be divorced; the *lips* say what the *heart* thinks, which is that *God raised* Jesus *from the dead;* only one so raised could be *Lord* (cf. 1: 4).

Lord is one of the names or titles given to God in the Old Testament. In the quotation from Joel 2: 32 used at 10: 13 *Lord* originally meant God; Paul takes it to mean Jesus. Lord was also a title which Gentiles commonly applied to their gods (see 1 Cor. 8: 5, 'there are many "gods" and many "lords"'); when the Roman emperors came to be thought of as divine (and they were so regarded in Paul's day) they were described with this title. The Christian, therefore, who calls Jesus *Lord* is putting him at least on the level of heathen gods (but really above them because the Christian only acknowledged one Lord, the heathen many); but he is doing much more, for he is actually putting Jesus on a level with God as known in the Old Testament (cf. 9: 5).

In verse 10 the order of *lips* and *heart* is reversed; in fact neither precedes the other: inward acceptance of what Jesus has done and outward acknowledgement of it should be simultaneous. The two halves of this verse are indeed parallel, for, as we have already seen (notes on 1: 16–17), *righteousness* and *salvation* are the same. Paul is not saying two different things but expressing one truth in two ways.

11–13. Paul takes up the two aspects of verse 10 and supports each with a quotation from Scripture. In verse 11 he uses Isa. 28: 16 (cf. Rom. 9: 33) and in verse 13, Joel 2: 32. He adds *everyone* to the quotation of Isa. 28: 16 to bring out the point he drives home in verse 12; this latter verse re-states what he said in 3: 22–3 (see the notes there) making the lack of distinction depend no longer on the fact that all men, *Jew and Greek* (Gentile), have sinned, but on the fact that there is one *Lord* for both and his righteousness is *rich* enough to include both. ✳

NO EXCUSE FOR ISRAEL'S FAILURE

How could they invoke one in whom they had no faith? 14
And how could they have faith in one they had never
heard of? And how hear without someone to spread the
news? And how could anyone spread the news without a 15
commission to do so? And that is what Scripture affirms:
'How welcome are the feet of the messengers of good
news!'

But not all have responded to the good news. For Isaiah 16
says, 'Lord, who has believed our message?' We conclude 17
that faith is awakened by the message, and the message that
awakens it comes through the word of Christ.

But, I ask, can it be that they never heard it? Of course 18
they did: 'Their voice has sounded all over the earth, and
their words to the bounds of the inhabited world.' But, I 19
ask again, can it be that Israel failed to recognize the message? In reply, I first cite Moses, who says, 'I will use a
nation that is no nation to stir your envy, and a foolish
nation to rouse your anger.' But Isaiah is still more daring: 20
'I was found', he says, 'by those who were not looking for
me; I was clearly shown to those who never asked about
me'; while to Israel he says, 'All day long I have stretched 21
out my hands to an unruly and recalcitrant people.'

* Paul drives home the point that responsibility for Israel's
failure lies with no one but the Jews themselves. God did everything to ensure that they should have their opportunity; they
heard the Gospel but rejected it.

14–15. God sends his *messengers* to *spread the news* of Jesus
that men may *hear*, *have faith* and so *invoke* the name of Jesus
and be saved' (verse 13). Yet the Jews do not *invoke* the name.

Has then one of the links of this chain been broken? Certainly not! Preachers have been sent by God—Paul confirms it with a quotation from Isa. 52: 7—and the Jews have heard the message (10: 18–21). The failure must lie in their response to what they heard, i.e. the failure lies in the Jews themselves.

16–17. Paul draws the conclusion (verse 16) and confirms it with another quotation. This comes from Isaiah (53: 1) near the beginning of one of the passages in which Isaiah prophesies about God's servant who would suffer; the Jews have not *believed* the *message* about the Christ who suffers.

not all: of course some Jews *responded*—Paul himself, Peter and the original disciples and many more (see Acts 2: 41).

message: in the original this means 'that which is heard' and thus links verse 17 more directly to verse 14; it also brings out the point that it is the failure of the Jews to hear properly rather than any failure in the content of the message that has led them to reject Jesus. What is heard is *the word of Christ*, i.e. the preacher has the authority of Christ behind his words, he speaks about Christ and what he says is in conformity with what Christ says about himself.

18. Paul rejects the excuse that Israel may not have *heard* the Gospel preached. The quotation is from Ps. 19: 4, in which all creation knows and praises its Creator. Praise is now given to God by men from *all over the earth* through the spread of the Gospel. Rome has heard; Israel must therefore have heard.

19–21. Paul rejects the excuse that Israel may not have been able to understand what is preached. If a *foolish nation* (the Gentiles, who had none of the advantages of Israel—9: 4–5) could understand, Israel ought to. Equally if those who were not concerned about the true God, who *were not looking for* him nor *asking about* him, found him through his disclosure of himself in Jesus, Israel ought to. God has indeed continually *stretched out* his *hands* with the gift of righteousness to the Jews but they have pushed them away. The quotations come from Deut. 32: 21 (verse 19), Isa. 65: 1 (verse 20), and Isa. 65: 2 (verse 21).

Verse 19 has the first explicit mention of *Israel* in this chapter; though Paul has had the Jews in mind throughout, he now makes it perfectly clear in case any Jew should have failed to grasp it. *Isaiah* is *daring* because what he says goes against the whole drift of Jewish thought—that their privileges ensured for the Jews that they would always be God's people and that the Gentiles would always be rejected.

The *envy* and *anger* of the Jews at the Gentiles is taken up in chapter 11: it is part of God's plan and will lead eventually to Israel's salvation. ✲

THE REMNANT

I ask then, has God rejected his people? I cannot believe it! **11** I am an Israelite myself, of the stock of Abraham, of the tribe of Benjamin. No! God has not rejected the people 2 which he acknowledged of old as his own. You know (do you not?) what Scripture says in the story of Elijah—how Elijah pleads with God against Israel: 'Lord, they have 3 killed thy prophets, they have overthrown thine altars, and I alone am left, and they are seeking my life.' But what does 4 the oracle say to him? 'I have left myself seven thousand men who have not done homage to Baal.' In just the same 5 way at the present time a 'remnant' has come into being, selected by the grace of God. But if it is by grace, then it 6 does not rest on deeds done, or grace would cease to be grace.

What follows? What Israel sought, Israel has not 7 achieved, but the selected few have achieved it. The rest were made blind to the truth, exactly as it stands written: 8 'God brought upon them a numbness of spirit; he gave them blind eyes and deaf ears, and so it is still.' Similarly 9 David says:

> 'May their table be a snare and a trap,
> Both stumbling-block and retribution!
> 10   May their eyes be darkened so that they do not see!
> Bow down their back for ever!'

✻ If Israel has failed to accept God's message and has turned out to be unfaithful, and if some of the Gentiles have accepted it and are now God's people, does this mean that God is no longer concerned with Israel? It is with this question that Paul is occupied throughout chapter 11. In 11: 1–10 he argues that not all the Jews have been unfaithful and that both the unfaithfulness of the majority and the faithfulness of the minority are part of God's plan of salvation.

1. *Then*: Paul's argument in chapter 10 seems to indicate clearly that Israel has failed and that therefore *God* should *reject his people*. Has he done so? Paul has already formally denied that he had (3: 3–4). As a Jew, he could not possibly have accepted such an idea. In any case it is proved wrong by the very fact that he, a Jew, is also a Christian. There can be no doubt about his Jewishness: he belongs to the people with whom God made his covenant (an *Israelite*—see on 9: 4–5); he was born a Jew and could trace his descent back through his own *tribe* (*Benjamin*) to *Abraham* himself. And there can be no doubt that he as a Christian still belongs to God's *people*.

2–4. Paul now makes a strong affirmation out of the words of his question in verse 1: *God has not rejected* Israel (the words of the first half of verse 2 are a quotation from Ps. 94: 14 and 1 Sam. 12: 22). He could not, for he 'knew his own before ever they were' (8: 29). The words translated *he acknowledged of old as his own* are identical in the original with the words just quoted from 8: 29 and Paul is obviously recalling what he said there. If God has 'known' them then he is bound in the end to give them 'his splendour' (8: 30) and so they cannot be finally rejected.

Moreover if one man (Paul) is saved, more will be. This is proved from the example of *Elijah* who, fleeing from persecution and in despair, cried out to God that he was the only faithful man left in Israel. God told him (an *oracle* means here a message from God) that there were *seven thousand* others who had not turned to heathen worship (1 Kings 19: 1–18). *Baal* is the title of a Canaanite deity—actually it means simply 'lord', 'master'; in the Old Testament *Baal* appears as a rival to God.

5–6. The 'seven thousand' are one instance of a conception which occurs repeatedly in the Old Testament (see the quotations in 9: 27–9): within the Israel which is often unfaithful there is always a faithful core, the 'remnant'. This is the 'true' (cf. 9: 6–7) people of God and, Paul implicitly argues, consists now of those Jews who have become Christians. It does not exist only because God in his *grace* has *selected* it. God's 'selective purpose' chose Jacob and not Esau 'even before they were born' (9: 10–13); so also in his freedom he has *selected* the *remnant*. Its members have not been picked because they were better than the rest of Israel; in that case their selection would have depended on their *deeds* and not on God's *grace*. Paul links up again here with what he said about justification; both man's justification and his selection depend, not on his own *deeds*, but on God's 'free *grace* alone' (3: 24); this is because God's choice took place before those whom he selected 'ever... were' (8: 29; cf. 9: 12).

7. If the *selected few* who are Christians are the true *Israel*, what of the remainder, who are the majority in Israel? Israel *sought* righteousness (cf. 9: 31) but only the 'remnant' *achieved* it. Just as Pharaoh was made 'stubborn' (9: 17–18), so Paul now asserts that *the rest were made blind to the truth*. It is astonishing, but it appears that Paul has set Pharaoh and the majority of Jews on the same plane in that both have been made blind by God (cf. verse 8). This may look as if God has given these Jews no chance: he selected some as the 'remnant' and made the remainder *blind*. Paul is not, however, writing about the salvation of individual men but about God's plan of salvation. God has *made* them *blind* so that he may win the Gentiles and in that way eventually win back all Israel (11: 25–7). In chapter 10 Paul

has, moreover, shown that Israel is responsible for its own failure.

8–10. Paul now verifies from the Old Testament what he has been arguing. Verse 8 is a combination of Isa. 29: 10 and Deut. 29: 4. Verses 9–10 are a quotation from Psalm 69: 22–3, which Paul, in common with the Jews of his day, believed was written by David himself. It has presumably been chosen by Paul because it is linked to verses 7–8 by the idea of blindness. We should not therefore press the details of the quotation.

table: this is obscure; it is perhaps a reference to the part that meals played in the religion of the Jews (e.g. eating sacrifices and the Passover); even these meals, on which they prided themselves, could be a snare and bring them down (*stumbling-block*—cf. 9: 32–3). ✳

Bow down their back is an ancient metaphor for being a slave.

for ever is later proved untrue in 11: 25–7 where Paul argues that all Israel is eventually saved.

THE GENTILE CHRISTIANS IN GOD'S PLAN

11 I now ask, did their failure mean complete downfall? Far from it! Because they offended, salvation has come to
12 the Gentiles, to stir Israel to emulation. But if their offence means the enrichment of the world, and if their falling-off means the enrichment of the Gentiles, how much more their coming to full strength!

13 But I have something to say to you Gentiles. I am a missionary to the Gentiles, and as such I give all honour to that
14 ministry when I try to stir emulation in the men of my own
15 race, and so to save some of them. For if their rejection has meant the reconciliation of the world, what will their
16 acceptance mean? Nothing less than life from the dead! If the first portion of dough is consecrated, so is the whole
17 lump. If the root is consecrated, so are the branches. But if

some of the branches have been lopped off, and you, a wild
olive, have been grafted in among them, and have come to
share the same root and sap as the olive, do not make your-   18
self superior to the branches. If you do so, remember that
it is not you who sustain the root: the root sustains you.

You will say, 'Branches were lopped off so that I might   19
be grafted in.' Very well: they were lopped off for lack of   20
faith, and by faith you hold your place. Put away your
pride, and be on your guard; for if God did not spare the   21
native branches, no more will he spare you. Observe the   22
kindness and the severity of God—severity to those who
fell away, divine kindness to you, if only you remain within its scope; otherwise you too will be cut off, whereas they,   23
if they do not continue faithless, will be grafted in; for it is
in God's power to graft them in again. For if you were cut   24
from your native wild olive and against all nature grafted
into the cultivated olive, how much more readily will they,
the natural olive-branches, be grafted into their native
stock!

* The failure of the Jews to accept God's salvation has meant
that the Gentiles received their opportunity. This should pro-
voke the Jews into seeing what they have missed so that they
are taken back into their place in God's people, but it should not
breed over-confidence in the Gentile Christians so that they
lose their position as part of God's people.

11–12. The question of verse 1 is restated; it has become all
the more acute because Paul argued in verses 8–10 that God has
made Israel blind to *salvation*. Does their *failure* mean that their
exclusion from salvation is *complete*? Paul vehemently denies
this, arguing that their very failure is part of God's plan, because
through it he has been able to *enrich* the *Gentiles* with *salvation*.
The story of Paul in Acts shows how he used to preach the

Gospel first to the Jews and then, when they rebuffed him, turn with it to the Gentiles. When the Jews in Pisidian Antioch opposed Paul and Barnabas they answered 'It was necessary . . . that the word of God should be declared to you first. But since you reject it and thus condemn yourselves as unworthy of eternal life, we now turn to the Gentiles' (Acts 13: 46; cf. 18: 6; 28: 28; and see pp. 4 f.).

Paul believes that by his taking the message to the Gentiles the Jews will be stirred to *emulation*, i.e. they will desire what they have rejected when they see others enjoying it (cf. 10: 19). For Paul the failure of Israel is only temporary; one day all *Israel* (at *full strength*) and not just a few will be back within God's people, and this in turn will *enrich* the *Gentiles* even more (cf. 11: 25–32). The salvation of the Gentiles helps the Jews, and that of the Jews in turn the salvation of the Gentiles. God loves equally both Jew and Gentile (cf. 10: 12) and the Gentiles are not merely tools by whom the salvation of the Jews is achieved.

13–15. These verses in large part repeat the thought of verses 11–12. Paul addresses his readers as *Gentiles,* as the majority of them were, because he is about to turn to their relationship with the Jews in the people of God. He can speak freely to them because he, though a Jew, is their special missionary and apostle (cf. Gal. 2: 7, quoted at 1: 1). All Paul can hope for at the moment is that *some of* the Jews—an individual here and another there —will be saved. Their full *acceptance* will come later. Indeed up to now only a few Jews, whether moved by *emulation* or not, have become Christians.

life from the dead may mean that (*a*) their full *acceptance* comes at the end of the world when the dead are raised to life again, or (*b*) it will be like a coming alive of those who are dead—the Jews pay no heed to God now and so are like dead people; some day they will pay heed and then they will really live.

16. With two short metaphors Paul introduces what he has to say about the place of the Gentiles in the people of God. The first is drawn from the Old Testament (Num. 15: 17–21): when the first grain of harvest had been ground and cooked it was pre-

sented as a sacrifice to God, so that the rest of the harvest when prepared as food (*the whole lump*) would be regarded as made holy and therefore fit for food. The second metaphor utilizes the fact that the nature and health of a tree depend on its *root*. Paul adds this second picture because he wants to compare individual members of the people of God to the tree's branches. As a people they are represented by the *whole lump* and the tree. The *first portion* and the *root* are the patriarchs (cf. 9: 5). The underlying thought—that the nature of the whole people is determined by one or more individuals—is akin to what we found in 5: 12–21 (see especially pp. 63–4). If the patriarchs were *consecrated*, i.e. separated as the people of God because he selected them, then the rest of his people is *consecrated* also.

17–18. Paul now elaborates the second metaphor of verse 16. The tree is specified as an *olive*, an image often used among the Jews to denote Israel. Some Jews have rejected Jesus and been rejected by God, i.e. *lopped off*, and Gentiles, branches of the *wild olive*, who have accepted God's righteousness through faith have been brought (*grafted*) into the people of God. These Gentiles thus draw on the *root* and *sap* of the original tree: the whole Jewish heritage of the Old Testament and its promises is now theirs, in particular the patriarchs are their patriarchs (Abraham is 'the father of all', 4: 11–12). They are dependent on this heritage which *sustains* them; they cannot cut themselves off from it. The Old Testament and its people are as much a part of the life of the Christian church as is the New Testament.

Paul's picture is contrary to normal horticultural practice in which branches from a cultivated tree are grafted on to the stock of a wild tree to produce good fruit and are not cut off later (cf. verse 21). Clearly Paul is aware of the peculiarity of his picture because he speaks of it as 'against all nature' (verse 24), but he is forced into it by the nature of his argument.

19–21. Paul emphasizes a point he has already made in verse 18—'do not make yourself superior to the branches'. Some of the Gentiles apparently looked down on the Jews who had rejected Jesus and who were therefore *lopped off*. Paul does not say why the Gentile Christians were acting like this: it may have been a touch of anti-semitism, which already existed in the pre-Christian world but for which there is no place in the Christian church, or a general feeling of superiority, i.e. *pride*, because they can now lay claim to the Jewish heritage. It was such a feeling of superiority which led to the exclusion (being *lopped off*) of the Jews from the people of God; they were proud of having the law and keeping it (3: 27-8) and did not think they needed the righteousness that comes through faith in Jesus (3: 26). The Gentile Christian may have begun by accepting this righteousness but if he goes on to pride himself that his position is secure because he has been *grafted in*, his faith will disappear and God will not *spare* him. *Faith* and *pride* are mutually exclusive (3: 27-8). Membership of the people of God does not rest on what a Christian does, not even on the fact that he has faith, but on what God does for him in giving Jesus to right wrong (1: 17).

22. The warning is continued and the responsibility of Jewish and Gentile Christians stressed. God will act in *kindness* or *severity* as they live by trust in himself or without it.

23-4. Paul gives the picture another strange twist: branches which have been *cut off* may be *grafted in again*. The branches which originally belonged to a tree—so he now argues—will be grafted more easily to it; thus the Jew who belonged to the people of God will be reunited more easily to that people. Paul is now back with his main point, not the position of the Gentiles in the people of God, but the position of the Jews—and back with his great desire that the Jews should *be grafted* again *into their native stock* (cf. 9: 3-4; 10: 1). ✳

A DEEP TRUTH

25 For there is a deep truth here, my brothers, of which I want you to take account, so that you may not be complacent about your own discernment: this partial blindness has come upon Israel only until the Gentiles have been

admitted in full strength; when that has happened, the 26
whole of Israel will be saved, in agreement with the text
of Scripture.

> 'From Zion shall come the Deliverer;
> He shall remove wickedness from Jacob.
> And this is the covenant I will grant them,   27
> When I take away their sins.'

In the spreading of the Gospel they are treated as God's 28
enemies for your sake; but God's choice stands, and they
are his friends for the sake of the patriarchs. For the gracious 29
gifts of God and his calling are irrevocable. Just as formerly 30
you were disobedient to God, but now have received
mercy in the time of their disobedience, so now, when you 31
receive mercy, they have proved disobedient, but only in
order that they too may receive mercy. For in making all 32
mankind prisoners to disobedience, God's purpose was to
show mercy to all mankind.

✶ Paul sums up the argument of chapters 9-11 and shows that
'the word of God' has not 'proved false' (9: 6). The Jews,
though they have rejected God's ways, are not beyond the
reach of his mercy and will one day be again brought completely into his people.

25-6. *For there is a deep truth here*: Paul has used the picture of
the olive tree (11: 16-24) in order to show that eventually the
Jews will again be grafted in. It is this which he now clarifies as
the *deep truth*. God accomplishes it in three stages: (i) the *partial
blindness* of the Jews: part of Israel, the 'remnant', is saved, part
has rejected God and is blind; (ii) the salvation of the *Gentiles*;
(iii) the salvation not just of the 'remnant' but of *the whole of
Israel*. Throughout this section Paul stresses that each stage leads
necessarily to the next.

When Paul says that *the whole of Israel will be saved* he does not necessarily imply that every Jew will be saved; he means that the nation as a whole will be restored. As a whole it has rejected God; its leaders contrived the death of Jesus and the people did nothing to save him; the great majority of them later refused to accept Jesus as their Messiah when Paul and the other Christians preached about him. There were of course exceptions, e.g. Paul and the disciples. When the *whole of Israel* is saved this will be changed; Paul does not make it clear whether there will still be exceptions or not, whether every single Jew will be saved or if some will not; this is not really the issue he is discussing here. In a similar way the *full strength* of the *Gentiles* means the generality of Gentiles, without implying that every Gentile will or will not be saved. Indeed the Gentiles are again warned (cf. II: 18–23) against any complacent reliance on their present membership in God's people.

26–7. Paul confirms this *deep truth* with a combination of quotations from Isa. 59: 20–1; Ps. 14: 7; Isa. 27: 9. Israel is to be saved by a *Deliverer* (Jesus) who has come once and will come again from Zion (originally the name for the hill on which Jerusalem was built, but here it means heaven); thus Israel will be brought into a new relationship (*covenant*) with God. The statement of 9: 6 is finally affirmed: God's promises still stand and Israel is not finally cast out of God's people.

28–9. The 'deep truth' (verse 25) is re-expressed. The unbelief of the Jews has led God to treat them as *enemies* and has thus benefited (*for your sakes*) the Gentiles. Yet in the final issue the Jews are God's *friends* because he cannot really be anyone's enemy and because his choice of Israel cannot be changed. He made promises to the *patriarchs* for themselves and their descendants ('And the Lord appeared unto Abram, and said, "Unto thy seed will I give this land",' (Gen. 12: 7)). These promises, in particular that of their calling, i.e. that God chose them as his people, not that they first chose him, are *irrevocable*: nothing can affect them, not even Israel's disobedience. Thus Israel once called is not abandoned, though in God's plan it may be temporarily set aside.

30–1. The explanation of the 'deep truth' is continued. The destiny of Jews and Gentiles is interlocked.

Many of the better manuscripts insert a 'now' between *may* and *receive mercy* in verse 31. This is so difficult to explain that it is probably original; copyists left it out when they could not understand it. By it Paul may have meant that in comparison with the long story of the Jews the end of the world was coming very quickly (and there is plenty of evidence that Paul thought so: in 1 Thess. 4: 15 he speaks of himself as being 'left alive until the Lord comes', cf. 1 Cor. 15: 51–2 and Rom. 13: 11–14); thus now, in the very immediate future, the Jews would be saved. Alternatively he may have meant that God was not postponing his *mercy* towards the Jews to some distant future date; even now he is showing *mercy* to them because some are being saved; this view is supported by verse 32, if we understand it to mean that God shows both wrath (cf. 1: 18–32) and mercy to all men at the same time, but that his ultimate purpose is to have mercy on men—to right wrong and give life (1: 17).

32. Here is the conclusion to the whole argument: God treats all men in the same way (cf. 3: 22–3; 10: 12). The stubbornness (9: 17–18) and blindness (11: 7–11) which he inflicts on Gentile and Jew alike, so that they are disobedient, does not have as its purpose their destruction; it is part of his plan to bring them *mercy*. Paul has laboured in his letter to prove that God is bringing mercy to both Jew and Gentile. ✳

GOD IS TO BE PRAISED FOR HIS PLAN
OF SALVATION

O depth of wealth, wisdom, and knowledge in God! How 33
unsearchable his judgements, how untraceable his ways! Who knows the mind of the Lord? Who has been his 34
counsellor? Who has ever made a gift to him, to receive 35
a gift in return? Source, Guide, and Goal of all that is—to 36
him be glory for ever! Amen.

* Paul has reached the end of his argument and he breaks out into praise of God for his wonderful mercy in contriving a way to save both Jew and Gentile despite their disobedience.

33-5. The plan of God for man's salvation far surpasses anything man could think out for himself. If God had not made it known in the story of the Jews and by sending his son Jesus, neither Paul nor any one else would ever have been able to discover it. Even then Paul's explanation does not exhaust the understanding of what God has done for men in his mercy. No one can hope to understand God fully.

wealth: the same word and with the same meaning as 'rich' in 10: 12. Verses 34-5 are quoted from Isa. 40: 13 and Job 41: 11.

36. *Source, Guide, and Goal of all that is*: a fairly common phrase used by both Jews and Greeks in praise of God. By it Paul means that the story of mankind began with God, is shaped by God and will reach the end which God has designed for it. *Amen* is the translation of a Hebrew word which was used as a response to a prayer or oath spoken by someone else; it means 'truly' or 'surely'. Paul thus gives his assent to the words he has quoted. He may not fully understand God's plan, he doubts if any man can, but he himself is prepared to accept it and praise God for it. Even if we cannot fully understand, yet we can praise.

And there is much that is difficult to understand in chapters 9-11. They imply throughout that God has a plan. In order to carry it out he selects some men (e.g. Isaac, Jacob); he makes others stubborn (Pharaoh) and blind (all Israel); he cuts some out of his people and he grafts others in. It is even said that he arranged beforehand ('fore-ordained') some men to 'be shaped to the likeness of his Son' (8: 29-30). Does not all this conflict with any conception of human responsibility? As if Paul wishes us to know that he is not unaware of this, he shows in chapter 10 that Israel was responsible for its own failure to accept its Messiah, and in 11: 17-24 he implies that Gentiles might lose their position in the people of God through pride. We are probably more perplexed by the idea that God should have a predetermined plan to which he appears to make men conform than by the idea of man's freedom and responsibility; yet this has not always been so. Many great Christians have drawn strength from the belief that they fitted into God's plans, that their salvation did not depend on their own ability as responsible human beings to keep God's law but that he had selected them; thus they could feel certain that he would preserve them through all the trials and troubles of their lives.

Taken in this way Paul's teaching in 8: 29–30 and chapters 9–11 is in accordance with his teaching on justification (cf. 9: 16, 30–3; 10: 1–6). Both imply that God does not save men because of what they are (members of his people) or what they do (keep his law). A man is justified through faith by what God has done in Christ; it is an act of 'God's free grace alone' (3: 24). A man is selected or fore-ordained 'by the grace of God' (11: 5), and this also is related to what God does in giving Jesus. 'In Christ he chose us before the world was founded' (Eph. 1: 4; Ephesians may not have been written by Paul; if it was not, it was written by someone who was very close to him in thought and wished to continue his teaching). We saw in 5: 12–21 that what had happened to the head of the new humanity affects all who are its members; so when God is said to select men it is because he has first of all selected Jesus; just as men die and rise with Jesus (6: 1–11), so they are also selected with him. Paul's teaching about God's selection and fore-ordination of men is thus part and parcel of his teaching about Jesus; it is not just an abstract philosophical idea.

We need to note also that Paul is not enunciating a general theory that everything that happens takes place in accordance with a predetermined plan of God; he is writing about what happens to men in relation to the salvation of the world. He is not even saying that God 'selects' men for salvation. As we have seen throughout chapters 9–11, when God chooses men like Jacob he does so in order that he may advance his purpose, which is 'to show mercy to all mankind' (11: 32); he selects men to serve him in that purpose. If he knew them before ever they existed it was not in order that they might enjoy eternal bliss but that they might 'be shaped to the likeness of his Son' (8: 29-30) who was crucified; and Paul goes on to speak of the perils, affliction and persecution that face them (8: 35-6). The opposite is also true: when God makes men stubborn (9: 17-18) or blind (11: 7-10, 25) this is not in order that he may blame them and punish them but that he may 'show mercy to all mankind' (11: 32). There is no idea that God chooses men to damn them. Whenever Paul speaks of God as punishing men (cf. 1: 18-32) it is because of sins that they have committed as responsible human beings.

Does this leave the problems unanswered? To some extent it does. Men still appear in part as puppets used by God for his own purposes, and this difficulty is not entirely met when we allow that the purpose is the good of the puppet and when we remember that the controlling God is the God who loves men enough to have given them his Son to die on the cross for them. Yet Paul cannot let this point go. It is of the very heart of his religion that God is in charge of the universe, planning and controlling all that happens, and that Jesus is at the centre of God's planning; it is equally of the heart of his religion that he, Paul himself, is responsible, and consciously responsible, for what he does. There is no easy solution to this apparent paradox. Paul is very much aware of it and knows that he cannot surrender either side; that is why he finishes by confessing (11: 33-6) that God's ways are far beyond man's understanding. In the history of Christianity one or other side has often been given up, and this has always led to a caricature of the Christian faith.

We can now look back and see how Paul has carried through the task he set himself in chapters 9-11, that is, to show that God's word does not change. The problem became acute for Paul because God's choice of Israel appeared overthrown by their rejection of Jesus. In 9: 6-29 he showed that God's promises must be correctly understood; they cannot be applied unreservedly to all the descendants of Abraham; God is free to

choose to whom they apply. Moreover, Israel as a whole has
turned against God and is completely responsible for any failure
to respond to God's gift of Jesus (9: 30 — 10: 21). Yet God has
not given up Israel; his way of working may appear round-
about, but he intends to bring Israel back through the conversion of the Gentiles (11: 1–32). Thus his word has not changed.
Paul quotes Scripture throughout, showing that there is more
to it than a simple promise to Israel and a simple approval of all
that Israel may do. So, if God's promise still stands for the Jews,
it stands also in relationship to justification. This, then, is God's
way of saving men. Paul is now free to go on and take up the
actual demands made on daily living by his teaching about a
God who rights wrong. ✳

Christian Behaviour

12: 1 — 15: 13

✳ In 12: 1 — 15: 13 Paul describes the kind of life which it is
expected Christians will live. This is not a change of subject: it
develops naturally from what has preceded. We have already
seen that what he said about being a Christian led him to demand from his readers a new type of life (e.g. 6: 12–14; 8:
12–13). In our present section he begins to explain in some detail
what this life is. After restating in the briefest of summaries his
reason for calling his readers to it (12: 1–2) he goes on to show
how they should treat one another and how they should act
towards those who are not Christians (12: 3 — 13: 14); he then
takes up one particular point which must have been causing
great strain in the relationships of the Christians in Rome with
one another (14: 1 — 15: 13). Paul does not give a systematic
treatment of behaviour deduced from some first principle
(e.g. that the greatest good of the greatest number should
always be sought); he does not work out Christian attitudes in

related areas of life in careful order: he deals directly with some
of the situations encountered most frequently by the Christians
of the first century. This discloses basic attitudes which are still
valid for Christians today. ✳

THE BASIS OF CHRISTIAN BEHAVIOUR

12 THEREFORE, my brothers, I implore you by God's
mercy to offer your very selves to him: a living sacrifice, dedicated and fit for his acceptance, the worship
2 offered by mind and heart. Adapt yourselves no longer to
the pattern of this present world, but let your minds be remade and your whole nature thus transformed. Then you
will be able to discern the will of God, and to know what is
good, acceptable, and perfect.

✳ Drawing on what he has said in the earlier chapters, Paul calls
on Christians to devote themselves entirely to discovering what
God's will is and to practising it.

1. *Therefore* refers back to the whole of the earlier part of the
letter. Throughout it Paul has spoken of *God's mercy*, love and
goodness; recalling this he *implores* them to *offer* their *very selves
to* God; the word he uses for *selves* (see on 6: 12–13) is one that
implies, not only an inner feeling of gratitude for *God's mercy*,
but also actual deeds and words expressing it. The *sacrifice* of
animals, grain, oil, etc., was central to ancient religion. In asking, then, for a *sacrifice* from his readers, Paul is taking up something they would know all about. But he asks for a *sacrifice* of a
different nature—their *very selves*: it is not enough for a
Christian to offer things, his possessions, his time, his talents, to
God; he must *offer* himself. Such a *sacrifice* is *living* because the
Christian possesses new life (5: 12–21; 6: 1–14); it is also *living*
in the sense that once an animal is sacrificed it is dead, but the
Christian's sacrifice of himself is a continuously living action.
The Christian is *dedicated* (see on 1: 6–7) as the Old Testament

sacrifice was expected to be (see on 15: 16). These qualities ensure its *acceptance* by God. Moreover, such a sacrifice is true *worship*, not consisting only of outward and formal actions as might happen in a church or temple service, but coming from the very depths of man's being (*mind and heart*) and pervading all he does; everything a Christian does can be *worship*. The word which lies behind the phrase *by mind and heart* also suggests that it is the kind of worship which a Christian offers when he is truly himself, when the Spirit dwells in him.

The translation of the N.E.B. footnote, '...acceptance, for such is the worship which you, as rational creatures, should offer', gives a slightly different sense; it implies that the service which Paul outlines here is the fitting worship for men whose lives, unlike those of animals, are guided by reason. The translation of the text is preferable.

2. The *pattern* of the lives of Paul's readers before they were Christians had followed that of *this present world*, i.e. the Old Age; 1: 18 — 3: 20 gave an indication of that *pattern* with its descriptions of sin among Gentiles and Jews. Now that Paul's readers belong to the New Age, the pattern must be changed and their lives must show the change: 12: 3 — 15: 13 will disclose what the new *pattern* is. Here Paul affirms that it must begin at the very centre of being—the *mind*. For Paul this denotes much more than a brain which can think logically and clearly when faced with a problem; the *mind* should both think out what is the *will of God* and make the decision to obey it. Thus the *whole nature*, and not just the thinking process alone, is *transformed*.

From 12: 3 Paul goes on to say what *the will of God* is. It may be objected that when Paul tells his readers to obey the will of God he is going back on his earlier teaching that what a man does cannot save him, and is now arguing that men should keep the law. We have already seen that Paul was sometimes accused of being indifferent to the behaviour of a man who had faith (6: 1–14). The present objection is just the opposite. Like the other, however, it misunderstands what faith is. If one man trusts another, especially if he trusts a superior, he will express his trust by doing what the other wishes; thus our faith in God should naturally lead us to do what God wants. Again, if we are grateful to God for his mercy, then we will be willing to obey him. Such obedience does not save a man; it flows naturally from the new situation created by the action of God in righting wrong by Christ, and man's response in faith to that action. 'The only thing that counts is faith active in love' (Gal. 5: 6).

But can a man do what God wants? Earlier Paul wrote as if man was so caught up in a web of sin (1: 18 — 3: 20; 5: 12-21; 7: 7-25) that he could not do *the will of God*. Now, however, he is writing to those whose feet are set 'upon the new path of life' (6: 4), who have been 'emancipated from sin' (6: 18), who are 'united with Christ Jesus' (8: 1), and who are 'on the spiritual level' (8: 9). Already by their response to what God has done in Christ their *nature* is being *transformed*. Paul entreats them to allow that transformation to become obvious in whatever they think, say or do. Since they live in the New Age they should show the conduct appropriate to that Age. We can now see how much 12: 1-2 depends on the earlier part of the letter, and how essential is the point which Paul makes if he is to say anything at all about the behaviour God demands. *

SACRIFICE IN THE LIFE OF THE CONGREGATION

3 In virtue of the gift that God in his grace has given me I say to everyone among you: do not be conceited or think too highly of yourself; but think your way to a sober estimate based on the measure of faith that God has dealt to each of
4 you. For just as in a single human body there are many
5 limbs and organs, all with different functions, so all of us, united with Christ, form one body, serving individually as limbs and organs to one another.
6 The gifts we possess differ as they are allotted to us by God's grace, and must be exercised accordingly: the gift of

inspired utterance, for example, in proportion to a man's
faith; or the gift of administration, in administration. A 7
teacher should employ his gift in teaching, and one who has 8
the gift of stirring speech should use it to stir his hearers. If
you give to charity, give with all your heart; if you are a
leader, exert yourself to lead; if you are helping others in
distress, do it cheerfully.

＊ The Christian is to offer himself as a sacrifice: Paul now indicates what this means in the life of the congregation. The great
variety of responsibilities God lays on its members and the gifts
he gives them in order to fulfil these responsibilities must be
exercised in harmony for the benefit of all the members.

3. Paul as an apostle appointed by God has his own responsibility towards the church; God in his goodness has *given* him the
ability (*gift*) to exercise it; it includes the instruction of believers in the nature of what it means to be a Christian; Paul
now takes this up in regard to their conduct.

Others as well as Paul have 'gifts' (verse 6) to be used in the
service of the congregation. The danger is that they will be so
thrilled with them that they will become *conceited* and not use
them for the good of all, but to gather the admiration of others.
So, taking up the idea of the renewal of their 'minds' (verse 2),
Paul warns them to *think* soberly about themselves.

The measure of faith: the more a man responds to God in faith,
the more he really comes to understand not only God but also
himself, and so can come to a *sober estimate* of himself and the
capabilities and gifts God has given him.

4-5. Christians and their gifts are set together in a balanced
unity, like the *limbs and organs* of the human *body*. We have already seen that Paul has shown that the believer is *united with
Christ* (cf. 6: 3, 11; 8: 1 for the phrase) as a member of the new
humanity; now it is brought out that those who are *united with
Christ* are also *united* with one another and require therefore to
behave in such a way that their mutual unity is furthered. In

1 Cor. 12: 12–27 Paul expands this idea of Christians as joined together in the unity of a body and he argues that the *body* is the body of Christ; thus the Church is called 'the Body of Christ'.

6–8. Paul enumerates some of the activities in the congregation for which God has equipped men. He is not setting out a list of authorized ministries like bishop, priest, and deacon, or minister and elder. The list is not exhaustive and the different *gifts* cannot be rigidly demarcated from one another. The first four refer to more official activities, to people with obvious and definite responsibilities, e.g. the preacher or teacher. The last three show that to help those in need either by a gift of money or by some other material assistance is just as important as to preach or teach, and equally requires God's help to carry it out. Probably Paul has here in mind organized charity on the part of Christians for those in need within their own community. The very different kinds of activity are all necessary, so that the church should function as a unity; since they are all *gifts* of God no one should be conceited about his own but should use them in the limited sphere to which they apply. *Gifts*: the word behind this shows that Paul is not thinking so much of the talents with which a man is born as of new capabilities to serve others which appear in him when he becomes a Christian. Preaching is more than an inborn ability to speak clearly and eloquently; it involves understanding God's ways so that they can be explained to men; God helps some Christians so to understand. He will of course use existing natural talents by fitting his *gifts* to them.

In proportion to a man's faith: cf. 'the measure of faith' (verse 3). ✳

LOVE IN THE LIFE OF THE CHRISTIAN

9 Love in all sincerity, loathing evil and clinging to the good.
10 Let love for our brotherhood breed warmth of mutual affection. Give pride of place to one another in esteem.
11   With unflagging energy, in ardour of spirit, serve the Lord.

Let hope keep you joyful; in trouble stand firm; persist 12
in prayer.

Contribute to the needs of God's people, and practise 13
hospitality.

Call down blessings on your persecutors—blessings, not 14
curses.

With the joyful be joyful, and mourn with the mourners. 15

Have equal regard for one another. Do not be haughty, 16
but go about with humble folk. Do not keep thinking how
wise you are.

Never pay back evil for evil. Let your aims be such as all 17
men count honourable. If possible, so far as it lies with you, 18
live at peace with all men. My dear friends, do not seek 19
revenge, but leave a place for divine retribution; for there
is a text which reads, 'Justice is mine, says the Lord, I will
repay.' But there is another text: 'If your enemy is hungry, 20
feed him; if he is thirsty, give him a drink; by doing this
you will heap live coals on his head.' Do not let evil con- 21
quer you, but use good to defeat evil.

✳ Having dealt with the different ways in which Christians
may serve God in the life of the church, Paul shows what should
be their actions and attitudes in their more personal dealings
with one another (verses 9–13, 15–16) and with those who are
not Christians (verses 14, 17–21). A seemingly miscellaneous
group of instructions are held together by two key thoughts:
the Christian loves others and seeks to do that good which is the
will of God (12: 2).

In most of this passage Paul is probably employing material
which had been used from very early days in the church for the
instruction of new Christians in the way they should behave.

9. *Love in all sincerity*: this is almost a heading for all that follows, up to 15: 13. The Christian, having found out what God's

love for him is like, ought to be able to love his fellows. But love can very easily become insincere when it is seen as something that has to be shown: we may reason out what action love requires and may do it—but only in order to show others that we love, or to satisfy ourselves that we are doing our duty. When that happens the person who is helped is not loved in the way God loves us. The loving action will, of course, always be one in which *evil* is avoided and *good* is firmly grasped.

10. *love for our brotherhood*: at a time when a person who became a Christian stood in danger that his family would sever their connexions with him, it was good that he should at once find himself within a new family, the church, where he would discover a *warmth* of *affection*. As in any true family the members will not push themselves forward to get attention but will *give pride of place to one another in esteem*.

11. *With unflagging energy*, that is, in loving men and in seeking good.

in ardour of spirit: not just sheer enthusiasm; the *spirit* is man's spirit, but man's spirit as directed, dwelt in and stirred up by God's spirit (cf. 8: 9).

serve the Lord: when we love others Jesus is served. In the N.E.B. footnote another translation is noted for this last phrase, 'meet the demands of the hour'; though the English words of the translation are very different the original Greek words are similar and occur in many manuscripts. If we choose this rendering it does not mean that the believer is to do just what is convenient at the time; the 'hour' is the hour of the Last Day. Christians of Paul's time believed that they were very near to this (cf. on 11: 30–1; 13: 11–14); such a thought would spur their efforts to goodness, and the hope of its coming would make them joyful (verse 12).

12. *hope, trouble, prayer* were all related in 8: 18–27 (cf. 5: 3). Paul himself *persisted* in prayer for his churches: 'We always thank God for you all, and mention you in our prayers continually' (1 Thess. 1: 2; cf. Rom. 1: 9).

13. The emphasis in 12: 8 was on organized Christian

charity; here it must lie on individual acts of kindness and love, including gifts of money, of which one example is *hospitality*. All this is a way of putting into practice the conception of the church as a family (verse 10).

14. Many of the first Christians were persecuted because of their faith in Jesus. To *bless* someone means much more than to wish him good luck or good health; it is to hope and pray for his salvation. To *curse* is the opposite. Paul has a saying of Jesus in mind, 'Love your enemies; do good to those who hate you; bless those who curse you; pray for those who treat you spite-fully' (Luke 6: 28).

15. There is no Christianity without fellowship, and this means, as in a family, entering into those experiences of others which are deepest and mean most to them.

16. Fellowship is broken when people are *haughty*, will only associate with those they consider their equals, or keep re-membering their own wisdom. Jesus did not choose the great and learned as his disciples but went *about with humble folk*, and his followers should not be so conscious of the correctness of their own thinking or of the importance of their own gifts (cf. 12: 3–8) that fellowship is broken. The last sentence is a quotation from Prov. 3: 7 as given in the Septuagint.

17–18. The second half of verse 17 is a paraphrase of Prov. 3: 4. Since the Christian has a responsibility for the non-Christian it is important that the latter should see that the in-tentions of the Christian are honourable, and this they will be if the Christian loves him. In particular he will understand this if the Christian *lives at peace* with him. Paul recognizes that this may not always be *possible*, for the non-Christian may con-tinue to be antagonistic; persecution does not necessarily stop when the persecuted loves the persecutor. The Christian knows how to seek peace with his fellow-men because he has already found it with God (cf. 5: 1–11).

19. The believer having suffered at the hands of others may find he has an opportunity of *revenge*. If there is need for revenge it will be exercised by God, who can see the total picture of the

human situation; his prerogative of revenge should not be taken from him. Paul clinches the matter by quoting Deut. 32: 35. The time of *divine retribution* may be either at the last judgement (5: 9) or in the present (1: 18), perhaps exercised through the law court (13: 4).

20-1. If the Christian suffers evil from others he is not to remain inactive but to take positive steps to show goodness and love to them. In so doing he *will heap live* [i.e. burning] *coals on* his enemies' heads. The exact significance of this picture is lost to us; it cannot mean that by the Christian's loving action his enemy will be made to suffer more, now or at the last judgement; it means that in some way the enemy will be brought to know his wrong and to repent. Paul quotes Prov. 25: 21-2 but significantly omits the last line, 'and the Lord shall reward thee': the Christian does not love his enemy that God may do him (the Christian) good. Verse 21 sums up the thought of verses 17-20. ✻

OBEDIENCE TO CIVIL RULERS

13 Every person must submit to the supreme authorities. There is no authority but by act of God, and the existing 2 authorities are instituted by him; consequently anyone who rebels against authority is resisting a divine institution, and those who so resist have themselves to thank for the 3 punishment they will receive. For government, a terror to crime, has no terrors for good behaviour. You wish to have no fear of the authorities? Then continue to do right and 4 you will have their approval, for they are God's agents working for your good. But if you are doing wrong, then you will have cause to fear them; it is not for nothing that they hold the power of the sword, for they are God's agents 5 of punishment, for retribution on the offender. That is why you are obliged to submit. It is an obligation imposed not merely by fear of retribution but by conscience.

That is also why you pay taxes. The authorities are in God's 6
service and to these duties they devote their energies.

Discharge your obligations to all men; pay tax and toll, 7
reverence and respect, to those to whom they are due.

* The believer is a member of the new humanity, a new person
in a New Age; does this mean that he can disregard the way in
which ordinary life is lived so that he need pay no heed to
government and its officials since these may be considered as
belonging to the Old Age? Paul argues that such officials should
be obeyed because they have been appointed by God, and when
they are so obeyed God is served.

1. There appears to be a sudden break in subject matter at
this point. But from 12: 9 onwards the subject has been continually changing; such changes were typical of the ethical instruction of the early church and of many teachers of the
ancient world. This passage is, however, connected to the preceding one because the Christian has just been bidden (*a*) to
leave revenge to God, and the *supreme authorities* may be God's
agents in this, and (*b*) to love his enemies, and there will have
been times when persecuting officials will have seemed to act
like enemies. Since Paul does not write directly about this subject in his other letters he must have known it was important to
advise the Christians in Rome about it. There had been trouble
earlier between Jews and Christians, and the Government had
intervened (see pp. 5–6); Christians may have suffered then
and wanted to know what their future attitude should be if it
were to recur. Some Christians, believing that Jesus was their
king, may have argued that they were free from direction by
earthly rulers. As Rome was the central seat of government,
the church there may have been especially worried over this
problem.

the supreme authorities are the human agents of government:
the Emperor and his immediate officials in Rome, governors in
the provinces, and magistrates in towns and cities. Most Jews
accepted the view that these rulers held their position *by act of*

God; Wisd. 6: 3 is addressed to them: 'Your dominion was given you from the Lord, and your sovereignty from the Most High.' There was however a growing minority of Jews that believed that, since the Romans were Gentiles, taxes should be withheld from them and their authority resisted by force. Paul affirms that since rulers have been *instituted* by God it is the duty of the Christian to *submit* to their orders.

2–4. Paul draws out some of the consequences of verse 1. A stable order of civil society which is controlled by government authorities who are *God's agents* is something which is valuable; where there is anarchy everyone suffers. Stability requires that the Christian must accept the existing order of society by co-operating with it in his obedience; if he does so it works for his *good*—Paul is thinking here of social and material benefits, and perhaps also of freedom to preach the Gospel. When someone rejecting authority and refusing to fit into the pattern *resists*, he is punished, and this *punishment* is part of the action God takes against wrong. We saw in 1: 18–32 that his action, *retribution*, takes place now and is not necessarily postponed until the day of judgement. God punishes through the *punishment* by rulers. Civil authorities *hold the power of the sword*, i.e. they have the right to enforce their punishments even to the extent of putting men to death. Just as Paul accepted slavery as an institution and nowhere argued against it, so he accepts the death penalty; for him and his readers it was a fact which they had no power or opportunity to change. Our decision about it must be based on a much wider consideration of God's way for men than is supplied by Paul's present allusion.

5. Paul might have been wrongly taken up as suggesting that the only reason for obedience was *fear* of the consequences. He now makes it clear that the Christian's obedience should come willingly because the authorities are, he knows, appointed by God. The *obligation* should come from within himself (*conscience*) as much as from external restraint. The *conscience* of the Christian will have been 'remade' and so his submission will not be just conformity 'to the pattern of this present world' (12: 2).

6. Cf. the words of Jesus: 'Pay Caesar what is due to Caesar and pay God what is due to God' (Mark 12: 17).

7. *tax and toll* include every kind of financial levy, e.g. head tax, income tax, customs duty.

reverence and respect: Paul asks for more than outward obedience to rulers; he desires also an inner attitude of willing *reverence and respect* for them as 'God's agents' (verse 4).

Paul has been considering only a limited issue: the relationship of the Christian subject to the civil authorities. He has not therefore given us a full theory of the state. To begin to do so would have required also a discussion of the duty of the ruler; Jewish, Greek, and Roman teaching agreed in stressing his responsibility; the Jew held that God would remove the evil ruler. Paul does not deal with the duties of rulers, presumably because he wrote only for his immediate readers in Rome and none of them were rulers; the men among them would have been engaged in trade or been servants and slaves; women would not have been rulers at all.

But what Paul has written, because it is only partial, causes great difficulty. He lays down a universal principle: Christians ought to obey rulers. At the time of Paul's letter the Roman Empire was administered efficiently and with a real measure of justice for all; the provinces were enjoying a period of peace and settled government; Paul and his fellow missionaries were free to preach the Gospel—indeed the Roman authorities often protected them in this from the Jews who would have liked to stop them. But shortly after this period Christians began to be persecuted: Paul and Peter were martyred in Rome. In Revelation, which was written near the end of the first century, we find a changed attitude; rulers are regarded as having come under the control of evil powers: the beast (the representative of the Devil) 'was granted authority over every tribe and people, language and nation' and war was thereby waged on God's people (Rev. 13: 7). But even before the time of our letter Christians had run into conflict with Jewish authorities; their attitude is expressed in the answer of Peter and John to the order that they should cease preaching: 'Is it right in God's eyes for us to obey you rather than God?' (Acts 4: 19). This is not submission. Paul has failed to qualify his statements in the light of the fact that the authorities, though God's servants, may yet disobey God. He has considered only the case where, by and large, the government was working for the good of the people; if this is not so, then an attitude other than submission may be required. Nor has Paul envisaged the case of a democracy, in which the distinction between ruled and ruler is much less clear than it was in the Roman Empire; it is there part of the duty of an opposition party to work peacefully for a change of government. ✻

GOD'S WILL IS LOVE

8 Leave no claim outstanding against you, except that of mutual love. He who loves his neighbour has satisfied
9 every claim of the law. For the commandments, 'Thou shalt not commit adultery, thou shalt not kill, thou shalt not steal, thou shalt not covet', and any other commandment there may be, are all summed up in the one rule,
10 'Love your neighbour as yourself.' Love cannot wrong a neighbour; therefore the whole law is summed up in love.

✻ In its essential nature the law is God's call for obedience; to obey God is to love men and seek their good.

8. There again seems a more abrupt break than there actually is from the subject of 13: 1–7. The connexion lies in the word *claim*. It is possible to meet the *claims* ('tax and toll', verse 7) that rulers make on us, but there is a yet greater *claim*—that of *love*. It makes an unending demand. Paul begins as if he were going to restrict this to the love of Christians for one another (*mutual love*) but immediately widens it to a *love* for every man. As Jesus taught in the Parable of the Good Samaritan (Luke 10: 25–37), our neighbour is the person who needs our help; there is no limitation in respect of race, colour, belief or class.

9. From the Ten Commandments Paul quotes those which deal with relationships between people. The order in which they are given is not that of our English Bibles but follows what is found in some early copies of the Septuagint. If we wish to combine these separate commandments into one all-embracing sentence it is: *Love your neighbour as yourself.* This (quoted from Lev. 19: 18) was accepted as a true summary of the law by many Jews and by Jesus (Luke 10: 25–8). If this commandment is followed, then the others are necessarily carried out.

10. In keeping with the negative way in which the Ten Commandments are formed Paul first restates Lev. 19: 18 negatively and then moves on to reaffirm his central position— *the whole law is summed up in love. Love* not only contains every single commandment of God to serve men but surpasses them all because it sets no bounds to goodness. It would be possible to draw up a much vaster list of individual commandments than the few of verse 9 but no list would ever exhaust all that is contained in the command to *love.* In speaking of the *law* Paul is not taking back what he earlier said about it, that to keep it cannot save a man (3: 20). We have seen that the truest meaning of *law* is obedience to God's will (see pp. 26–8 and note on 3: 31). God's claim to our obedience never disappears; if we love, then we meet it. This, however, does not justify the Christian; it is because he is justified and knows what God's love is that he begins to understand how much God is asking from him and learns to practise love (cf. on 12: 1–2). ✳

AN URGENT APPEAL

In all this, remember how critical the moment is. It is time 11 for you to wake out of sleep, for deliverance is nearer to us now than it was when first we believed. It is far on in the 12 night; day is near. Let us therefore throw off the deeds of darkness and put on our armour as soldiers of the light. Let 13 us behave with decency as befits the day: no revelling or

drunkenness, no debauchery or vice, no quarrels or jeal-
14 ousies! Let Christ Jesus himself be the armour that you
wear; give no more thought to satisfying the bodily
appetites.

٭ Before taking up one special problem of conduct, Paul concludes what he has to say in a general way on Christian behaviour, just as he began (12: 1–2), with an appeal: since the end
of the world is coming soon Christians should not linger in sin
but take very seriously the call to show actual righteousness and
goodness in their lives.

   11. The *moment* is *critical* because it lies in the short period
between Christ's first coming and his second. His first coming
was his birth from Mary; he left earth again when he ascended
to heaven after his resurrection. His second coming will be his
return to execute God's judgement and to establish fully God's
kingdom and rule. This second coming, which will mean final
deliverance (cf. 5: 9), is appreciably *nearer* than when the readers
were converted. If Paul had conceived of it as centuries away he
could not have said that a few years had really brought it
nearer. There are other indications in his letters that he expected
it soon (see note on 11: 30–1).

   It is now over nineteen hundred years since Paul wrote; has
this taken the urgency from his words? In part, yes; but the
times may still be termed *critical* because, unlike the vast age
before Christ's first coming, we live in the period when 'God's
way of righting wrong' has been revealed (1: 17) and have to
decide whether we respond in faith or not. Moreover, since
Paul thought Christ was returning soon, he did not need to
point out how short our lives are and how brief the period in
which we can serve Christ in the world. Thus the *moment* for
each one of us may still be called *critical*. The urgency to offer
ourselves to God (12: 1–2) *in all this* (i.e. the exhortations of
12: 3 — 13: 10) has not changed, though the reasons for it may
appear different.

   12–14. The summons to 'wake out of sleep' (verse 11) evokes

the imagery of *night* and *day* (i.e. the *day* of Christ's second coming). In Jewish thought the Old Age was one of *night* and *darkness*, the New Age one of *light* and *day*. As we have seen, the Christian already lives in the New Age and yet awaits its full coming. So he ought even now to display the behaviour of the New Age by throwing *off the deeds of darkness* and putting on the *armour . . . of the light*. Here Paul introduces another metaphor—that of a change of clothing, perhaps suggested by the change made when we get up from bed for the *day*. The *bodily appetites* (detailed in verse 13) are put off; these *bodily appetites* are the same as the 'lower nature' (the same Greek word is used for both; see note on 7: 5–6); they are not merely *bodily*, for they include quarrelsomeness and jealousy (cf. note on 8: 12–13); they are whatever kind of conduct belongs to the Old Age. The *armour* which is put on is *Christ Jesus himself*. In Eph. 6: 13–18 the various parts of the *armour* are listed; they include a weapon, the sword, as well as protective armour, the coat of mail. In wearing Jesus Christ the Christian puts on the character and ways of Jesus (cf. 8: 29). Paul has used this idea elsewhere, writing 'Baptized into union with him [i.e. Christ], you have all put on Christ as a garment' (Gal. 3: 27). They are now called to let the world see the clothes they have already been given (cf. the argument at 6: 11–14, where they are bidden to show the new life which they already enjoy as risen with Christ). ✶

A DIFFICULT PROBLEM: 14: 1 — 15: 13
A DIVIDED CHURCH?

If a man is weak in his faith you must accept him without **14** attempting to settle doubtful points. For instance, one man 2 will have faith enough to eat all kinds of food, while a weaker man eats only vegetables. The man who eats must 3 not hold in contempt the man who does not, and he who does not eat must not pass judgement on the one who does; for God has accepted him. Who are you to pass judgement 4 on someone else's servant? Whether he stands or falls is his own Master's business; and stand he will, because his Master has power to enable him to stand.

5   Again, this man regards one day more highly than another, while that man regards all days alike. On such a point everyone should have reached conviction in his own
6   mind. He who respects the day has the Lord in mind in doing so, and he who eats meat has the Lord in mind when he eats, since he gives thanks to God; and he who abstains has the Lord in mind no less, since he too gives thanks to God.
7   For no one of us lives, and equally no one of us dies, for
8   himself alone. If we live, we live for the Lord; and if we die, we die for the Lord. Whether therefore we live or die,
9   we belong to the Lord. This is why Christ died and came to life again, to establish his lordship over dead and living.
10   You, sir, why do you pass judgement on your brother? And you, sir, why do you hold your brother in contempt?
11   We shall all stand before God's tribunal. For Scripture says, 'As I live, says the Lord, to me every knee shall bow and
12   every tongue acknowledge God.' So, you see, each of us will have to answer for himself.

✻ Having dealt with the more general aspects of Christian behaviour, Paul now turns to a problem which was perplexing the church in Rome (14: 1 — 15: 13). A minority was refusing to eat meat or drink wine (14: 21) and considered some days more important than others; the remainder thought these practices wrong. Paul is worried lest the church should be split over this and warns its members against criticizing one another.

It is difficult to be precise about the views and identity of the minority group. In some contemporary pagan religion and philosophy, and in some less normal forms of Jewish religion, abstinence from meat and wine was encouraged; it represented an ascetic tendency to subdue the desires of the body. Jews observed the Sabbath and various festivals throughout the year; some Jews also kept certain days each week as fast days. The group in Rome probably represented a mixture of these pagan and Jewish tendencies and was not too clearly defined. Later in the history of the church such views caused considerable trouble, developing into heresies which were condemned. At this stage Paul apparently does not regard the group as so dangerous that he needs to refute its views, as he had done in the case of those Jewish Christians who wished to insist that Gentiles should keep the law (cf. pp. 2–3). Obviously he disagrees with those who hold these opinions, but he is more concerned to see that the majority and minority live together as brothers in the church than to persuade the minority to change their views.

1. That some are *weak in* their *faith* is quite clearly the suggestion of those who disagree with them; they call them this because they think the *weak* persist in their practices in order to support their faith. This should not, however, lead to their exclusion from the fellowship of the church. They ought to be *accepted* as true members without first being argued out of their position on the *points* which are *doubtful*.

3–4. The danger is that those who see others held back by doubts will despise them, and those who have the doubts will be over-critical of those who seem to do whatever they like. Each group should remember that God has accepted the other, justified its members and received them into the church. Thus, where God does not judge and condemn, neither group should *pass judgement* on the other. In the final issue the members of both are only *servants* in God's household. Fellow servants do not judge one another and determine whether they *stand or fall* but abide by the decision of the *Master* of both. He, for his part, has already approved of those in either group and will therefore *enable* them to continue as Christians.

5–6. *day*: see introductory note to this section. It would have been easy for the church to draw up rules of conduct and decide which group was right; there would then be a danger that a man might think he was justified by keeping the rules and not by his response in faith to what God has done. Paul therefore prefers to say that each should be able to make up *his own mind* in the light of his knowledge of what the Christian faith is; such maturity is the sign of a remade mind (12: 2). When a man makes up his mind in the light of what he knows about his *Lord* and in fellowship with him, then his behaviour will be determined not by passing fashion or church rule but by fundamental *conviction*. That a man *has the Lord in mind* when he decides how to act excludes, naturally, certain beliefs and ways of behaving because they cannot be squared with what is known of God through Jesus; an opinion is not therefore necessarily to be allowed because it is sincerely held.

he gives thanks to God, that is, in the prayer of blessing to God before and after a meal; such prayers were a custom the Christians had taken over from the Jews. Obviously in the case of *meat* the strain between the two groups will have been felt most acutely at common meals; each should respect the attitude of the other as an attitude arising from his Christian faith. It will be seen that Paul nowhere argues the merits of the case as to which group is right or wrong; he is writing instead so that they may both be held together in respect for one another.

7–9. The *lordship* of Christ over the believer mentioned in verse 6 is now generalized. All conduct must take its reference from our service to Jesus whose claim to *lordship* over us comes from his death and resurrection.

10–12. If a man's conduct is offered in obedience to Jesus, then it is not for us to criticize him if he eats meat or to despise him if he abstains. We will not have to justify to God the conduct of others, but our own; the only judgement we should exercise is self-judgement so that *each of us* may *answer for himself*. The conclusion is driven home by the first few words of verse 13: 'Let us therefore cease judging one another.' Note Paul's use of *brother*; by it he reminds them of their mutual relationship within God's family (cf. 12: 10, 13). It is a lack of brotherliness which could divide them further. The quotation in verse 11 is a combination of Isa. 49: 18 with Isa. 45: 23 and is drawn from the Septuagint. ✻

CONSIDER YOUR BROTHER CHRISTIAN!

Let us therefore cease judging one another, but rather make 13 this simple judgement: that no obstacle or stumbling-block be placed in a brother's way. I am absolutely con- 14 vinced, as a Christian, that nothing is impure in itself; only, if a man considers a particular thing impure, then to him it is impure. If your brother is outraged by what you eat, 15 then your conduct is no longer guided by love. Do not by your eating bring disaster to a man for whom Christ died! What for you is a good thing must not become an occasion 16 for slanderous talk; for the kingdom of God is not eating 17 and drinking, but justice, peace, and joy, inspired by the Holy Spirit. He who thus shows himself a servant of 18 Christ is acceptable to God and approved by men.

Let us then pursue the things that make for peace and 19 build up the common life. Do not ruin the work of God for 20 the sake of food. Everything is pure in itself, but anything is bad for the man who by his eating causes another to fall. It is a fine thing to abstain from eating meat or drinking 21 wine, or doing anything which causes your brother's downfall. If you have a clear conviction, apply it to your- 22 self in the sight of God. Happy is the man who can make his decision with a clear conscience! But a man who has 23 doubts is guilty if he eats, because his action does not arise from his conviction, and anything which does not arise from conviction is sin.

✻ Paul addresses the majority who see no reason to abstain from meat or wine and who do not observe special days. While they are correct in this they ought to realize that food and the observance of days are relatively unimportant matters compared to the good of their fellow Christians who do not think as they do; they ought therefore to abstain if there is any risk of giving offence to their fellow Christians by partaking; the Christian belief of the minority will not then be imperilled.

13. *Let us therefore cease judging one another*: Paul sums up the preceding section.

but rather make. . . He turns specifically to the majority. The minority may be a source of amusement to the majority but they are never an *obstacle* or a *stumbling-block* to it; this however is precisely what the majority may be to the minority; this would happen if the minority were forced to conform to the majority against what they believed to be right (verses 20, 23), or if they become embittered by seeing the majority apparently sinning without a feeling of wrong; they might then even cease to be Christians (verse 15).

14. The majority are not of course in the wrong in what they believe; in God's eyes there is no difference between one kind of food and another and between one day and another—*nothing is impure in itself*. Here Paul says *as a Christian* what he could never have said as a Jew; for Jews believe in accordance with the law that certain foods, e.g. pork, are *impure*. Paul employs the word the Jews used to describe these forbidden foods; he does not mean they are unhygienic. In a discussion with the Jews Jesus had already made it clear that there were no *impure* foods when he said 'nothing that goes from outside into a man can defile him' (Mark 7: 18). Yet if a man is convinced that there are foods which he should not eat, even though his belief is false, then those foods are *impure* to him and he should not eat them. Paul thus recognizes the position of the minority and expects them to stand by it. No man should act contrary to his own clear beliefs (cf. 14: 5–6).

15–16. The case of the majority is somewhat different. To

abstain from food will hurt neither their beliefs nor their health. Their attitude should be *guided by love*. It is more important to *love* one's brother Christian than to enjoy the freedom (*good thing*) which every Christian has in respect of food. To exercise this freedom may result in the minority speaking *slanderously* against them and so sinning; or the minority may be *outraged* within themselves at what they consider the presumptuous actions of those who eat. Thus the majority may *bring disaster* to the minority; the latter may even go so far as to lose their Christian faith. The failure in *love* of the majority would thus destroy the Christian belief of the *man for whom* in love *Christ died* (5: 6–8; 15: 3).

17. Neither abstinence nor eating has much to do with the *kingdom of God*. The Jews believed that this would be established when the New Age came: God would rule men; they would live in his presence; food and drink would be unimportant. But the New Age has already come, though not yet completely; so with the *kingdom of God*. God's rule means that there will be and already is: (*a*) *justice*, i.e. the righteousness which God gives men when he sets right what is wrong and which then appears in their actual good deeds; (*b*) *peace*, i.e. the peace which God has created between himself and men (see on 5: 1–11) and which leads to peace between Christian and Christian; (*c*) *joy*, i.e. the joy which God's servants have when they see God's rule exist and evil defeated. The *Holy Spirit* was a gift expected in the New Age; already Christians possess this gift (cf. 8: 1–30).

18–19. The man who knows it is right to eat, and yet abstains because he loves his brother, serves God and God approves of him; love to God and love to one's neighbour go together. Within the Christian community this love for one's neighbour is seen in seeking *the things* that are for the good of the Church; *peace* between its members and thereby their mutual *building up*, i.e. growth in Christian knowledge and practice. It was for this that God gave the gifts of 12: 3–8. The community would be destroyed if men chose their own way without regard for others in it.

20. *the work of God*: what God has done and does through Jesus to make men members of the new humanity.

pure: verse 14 is here restated from a more positive angle.

bad: the man who ignores the minority and eats everything only harms himself, for what he does in such a situation is sinful and destroys his relationship with God.

21. Paul restates what he has been saying, generalizing it beyond the present issue.

22. The *conviction* of a Christian will arise from his response (i.e. his faith) to what God has done for him; this will lead him to find out what God wants him to do and to do it. When his mind is *clear* he ought to follow it out. This of course applies to both groups in the church. Equally, members of both are *happy* if they have no doubts about their abstinence and abstain, or about their eating and eat. No one will then be divided within himself about his conduct.

23. *But* if (and Paul now turns to the minority) they are convinced that eating is wrong and they eat, they will be divided in mind, doing what they know to be wrong, and will be *guilty*; their action will be *sin*, because it will not result from a desire to obey God but from a desire to conform to the general pattern by imitation of their brethren.

In the last part of the verse, *anything which does not arise from conviction is sin*, Paul is not defining the nature of wrong-doing in general but only in the case of the believer. He stands in the relationship of faith to God (and the word rendered *conviction* is the word usually translated 'faith'); in this response to God's goodness he begins to understand the way God wants him to behave; if, then, he goes against this understanding he sins. ✳

UNITY THROUGH LOVE

15 Those of us who have a robust conscience must accept as our own burden the tender scruples of weaker men, and
2 not consider ourselves. Each of us must consider his neighbour and think what is for his good and will build up the

common life. For Christ too did not consider himself, but 3
might have said, in the words of Scripture, 'The reproaches
of those who reproached thee fell upon me.' For all the 4
ancient scriptures were written for our own instruction, in
order that through the encouragement they give us we
may maintain our hope with fortitude. And may God, the 5
source of all fortitude and all encouragement, grant that
you may agree with one another after the manner of
Christ Jesus, so that with one mind and one voice you may 6
praise the God and Father of our Lord Jesus Christ.

In a word, accept one another as Christ accepted us, to 7
the glory of God. I mean that Christ became a servant of 8
the Jewish people to maintain the truth of God by making
good his promises to the patriarchs, and at the same time to 9
give the Gentiles cause to glorify God for his mercy. As
Scripture says, 'Therefore I will praise thee among the
Gentiles and sing hymns to thy name'; and again, 'Gentiles, 10
make merry together with his own people'; and yet again, 11
'All Gentiles, praise the Lord; let all peoples praise him.'
Once again, Isaiah says, 'There shall be the Root of Jesse, 12
the one raised up to govern the Gentiles; on him the
Gentiles shall set their hope.' And may the God of hope 13
fill you with all joy and peace by your faith in him, until,
by the power of the Holy Spirit, you overflow with hope.

* Paul completes his discussion (14: 1 — 15: 13) of the relationship between the two groups at Rome. Unity within the
church is important, and to preserve it members must be prepared not only to avoid pressing their own particular points of
view but also to help each other to live together in fellowship.
As an example for them he sets out Christ's love.

1-3. Paul now places himself alongside (*those of us*) the

majority in the church whose consciences see nothing wrong in meat or wine and who do not observe some days in a special way; by so associating himself with them he hopes to encourage them in a task which is not easy—to *accept* the *tender scruples* of the minority as a *burden*. Those who are *robust* can do this because indeed they are *robust,* using their strength not to *consider* themselves, i.e., to maintain their own position, but to bear the heavy weights others cannot. Accepting such *burdens* is difficult; it means more than the toleration of the strange ideas of others; it is the renunciation of our own freedom and a readiness to bear the *reproaches* of those who attribute wrong motives to us in what we do; it means self-denial. Jesus said, 'Anyone who wishes to be a follower of mine must leave self behind; he must take up his cross, and come with me' (Mark 8: 34). Paul refers to the example of Jesus by means of an Old Testament quotation (Ps. 69: 9; this Psalm was applied frequently by the early church to Jesus); he puts it on the lips of Jesus as summing up his whole attitude while he lived among men. The type of behaviour which Jesus displayed is relevant not only to the dispute in Rome but to all our dealings with our neighbours; through it we shall *build up the common life* (see note on 14: 19). Basically Jesus' attitude was one of love.

4. Paul digresses. He has just quoted from *the ancient scriptures* i.e. the Old Testament. It may be that some Gentile Christians, and the majority group would probably have been of largely Gentile origin, did not fully appreciate what the Old Testament could mean for them and regarded it only as a Jewish book. But it is for *our* (i.e. Gentile as well as Jewish) *instruction*. An example of the *encouragement* which these *scriptures* supply has just been given in verse 3. Ps. 69 foretells what treatment may be expected by the good man, i.e., in this context, the Christian of the majority party. He should not then take amiss the line of behaviour Paul directs him to adopt. It will enable him to *maintain* his *hope with fortitude*.

5-6. In a prayer, Paul picks up from verse 4 two words, *fortitude* and *encouragement*. The *encouragement* which the scriptures supply has its *source* in God. With it, and the *fortitude* God gives, those who differ will be able to live together in harmony. Despite the reference to *one mind* these verses do not necessarily imply that all differences of opinion will be overcome. It would be better if they were, but even if they are not those who differ should be able to 'accept one another' (verse 7), according to the example of Jesus indicated in verse 3, so that together they will be able to *praise* God. Only when Christians accept one another in fellowship is real worship possible.

7. Paul now addresses both groups (*one another*). Let them *accept* (cf. 14: 1, 3) each other into the full fellowship of all that goes on in the church as *Christ accepted* them. For he *accepted* all (even those who now claim to be 'robust', 15: 1) when they were 'powerless' (5: 6) or weak, before they became Christians; at that time all of them were 'weak'.

8-12. Paul moves on to what we have seen was the great division within the early church (cf. pp. 2-3); he does this perhaps because the scruples of the minority partially resemble the position of the Jewish Christians. If, then, the majority find it difficult to accept the weak in faith (14: 1) let them remember that Christ became a Jew to serve *the Jewish people*—and the Jews had scruples in regard to food and the keeping of the Sabbath, etc., which seemed much more peculiar to other peoples than would the scruples of the minority in Rome. Jesus was a Jew in order that God's faithfulness (*truth*) in his *promises* of salvation made to the *patriarchs* for the Jews might be fulfilled and in order that God's *mercy* in saving the Gentiles might be realized (see chapters 9-11).

The Old Testament quotations imply that Jews and Gentiles will together praise God under one leader, *the Root of Jesse*, i.e. Jesus, as the two groups in Rome ought to be doing (cf. verses 5-6). The quotation in verse 9 is from Ps. 18: 49, in verse 10 from Deut. 32: 43, in verse 11 from Ps. 117: 1, and in verse 12 from Isa. 11: 1 combined with Isa. 11: 10.

the Root of Jesse: this phrase was understood to imply that the Messiah would be a descendant of David, whose father was

Jesse; in 1: 3–4 we have already seen that Jesus was taken to be such a descendant of David.

13. Paul prays again for his readers (cf. verses 5–6). *Hope* is emphasized. Its source is God (*the God of hope*) and by it men are able to forget the divisions of the past by looking to what God promises for the future (cf. on 5: 1–2). Paul prays also for *joy and peace* because these are so easily destroyed by division; he expects all these gifts to come *by the power of the Holy Spirit* (cf. 14: 17). Their response in *faith* to what God has done for them in righting wrong enables them to receive his gifts of *joy*, *peace*, and *hope*—just as anyone benefits from the friendship of some good person he trusts.

This completes Paul's section on how Christians should behave. It has its origin in the response of the Christian to what God has done for him (12: 1–2); in gratitude he puts himself at God's disposal. As God has loved him, so love must govern his attitude to others. The centrality of love is made explicit in 13: 8–10, but also underlies the collection of individual demands made in 12: 3–21 and the detailed exposition of one particular problem (14: 1 — 15: 13). It is because Christ loved that his example is relevant to what we do (15: 3, 7). The Christian's love for others is not then the reason why God justifies him (if this were true Paul's earlier arguments in 3: 21 — 4: 25 would be negatived) but issues from that justification. Paul would have queried the justification of one who had not begun to love, though equally he would never have expected perfection in love.

Although love should govern all Christian behaviour this does not mean that Paul sees it as a principle or axiom from which there can be deduced a system of ethics to meet every situation in life. The almost haphazard nature of Paul's teaching, consisting in a succession of seemingly unrelated general precepts (12: 3–21), forbids such a conclusion. The very nature of love also renders it impossible to deduce a code of behaviour from it; once a detailed rule is laid down men act in obedience to it rather than out of love for the one in need of help. So, as actual situations occur in which they have to act, Paul expects his readers to learn for themselves what love is. In the one instance in which he has attempted to give detailed guidance (14: 1 — 15: 13) he has formulated no rules but has appealed to the party which is in the right, so far as its thinking goes, to consider in love the others and to embrace them within the warmth of full Christian fellowship; Paul has been more concerned with holding the church together than with adjudicating who was in the right. Because love by its nature forbids the construction of a detailed code of behaviour, what Paul says about it can be applied to our situations, which are often so very different from those of his original readers. For us too the whole demand of God 'is summed up in love' (13: 10). Yet since so many of his readers came from a pagan background in which the meaning of love was not fully understood, Paul felt it necessary to give some guidance as to the way in which one who loves will act.

The main argument of the letter, which began with 1: 16–17, ends at 15: 13. Paul has still, however, some matters of a more personal nature to raise with the Christians at Rome. ✳

PAUL JUSTIFIES HIS LETTER

My friends, I have no doubt in my own mind that you 14 yourselves are quite full of goodness and equipped with knowledge of every kind, well able to give advice to one another; nevertheless I have written to refresh your 15 memory, and written somewhat boldly at times, in virtue of the gift I have from God. His grace has made me a 16 minister of Christ Jesus to the Gentiles; my priestly service is the preaching of the gospel of God, and it falls to me to offer the Gentiles to him as an acceptable sacrifice, consecrated by the Holy Spirit.

Thus in the fellowship of Christ Jesus I have ground for 17 pride in the service of God. I will venture to speak of those 18

things alone in which I have been Christ's instrument to
19 bring the Gentiles into his allegiance, by word and deed, by
force of miraculous signs and by the power of the Holy
Spirit. As a result I have completed the preaching of the
20 gospel of Christ from Jerusalem as far round as Illyricum. It
is my ambition to bring the gospel to places where the very
name of Christ has not been heard, for I do not want to
21 build on another man's foundation; but, as Scripture says,

'They who had no news of him shall see,

And they who never heard of him shall understand.'

∗ With the main argument of the letter complete, Paul, returning (cf. 1: 1–15) to more personal matters, explains why he
has written to a church which he neither founded nor has ever
visited.

14–16. *My friends*: he begins intimately and warmly, as to
fellow members of the Christian family; *friends* renders the
word for 'brothers' in Greek. They did not really require his
letter, for with their own *goodness* (i.e. dealing in love with one
another) and *knowledge* (i.e. understanding of God's truth and
actions) they would have been able to work out a solution for
their particular problems. Paul therefore explains why he has
written to them; he has two reasons: (1) He is *refreshing* their
memory; there is nothing basically new in what he writes; it was
already known to them through the instruction in the Christian faith and life which was common to all parts of the early
church; (2) God has given him a special position in relation to
the *Gentiles* as the *minister of Christ Jesus* to them (cf. pp. 2–5 and
notes on 1: 1 and 11: 13). This position is also a *gift* from God
(see on 1: 5; 12: 3) and in writing he is only fulfilling the gift
with its accompanying obligation. On these grounds he excuses
himself if parts of his letter have appeared *somewhat bold*. He
does not say in what parts he may be thought to have gone too
far, but perhaps he has in mind what the two groups referred
to in 14: 1 — 15: 13 will say about his criticisms of them.

Paul describes his responsibilities towards the Gentiles in terms that were used of those (*priests*) who directed the worship and life of the temple at Jerusalem and of those who served in heathen temples. They offered *sacrifices:* he now *offers the Gentiles.* In 12: 1–2 they were implored to offer themselves as a sacrifice; Paul now looks on himself as presenting their sacrifice to God. According to the Old Testament any animal that was offered in sacrifice had to be pure, i.e., physically perfect, otherwise it was not *acceptable* to God. Believers are pure because they have been *consecrated* (see on 1: 7; 12: 1; *consecrated* and 'dedicated' come from the same Greek root). Equally we might say that they are *acceptable* because they have been justified, their sins forgiven, so that they are pure. The *Spirit* of God dwells in them (8: 9) and is termed the *Holy* Spirit; the word *Holy* is again the same as *consecrated* and 'dedicated'; so they are *consecrated* by the holiness dwelling in them. Again, as we have seen in chapters 9–11, Christians are the People of God, and in the Old Testament God's people are always a holy or *consecrated* People. Thus believers, by the very fact that they are members of God's people, are *acceptable* sacrifices because they are holy. We can see here how much of Paul's thinking interlocks. Just as he had earlier argued that men cannot put right the wrong in themselves, so now, quite consistently, he does not consider that they can present themselves as suitable sacrifices to God by virtue of their good and holy lives (cf. on 6: 17–22). Just as God rights wrong, so he also consecrates.

17–19. If what Paul has written sounds a little like boasting then he will defend himself; he has not acted apart from Christ Jesus but in his *fellowship;* and it has been God's work, for God called him to be *Christ's instrument to bring the Gentiles to allegiance.* He has indeed been his instrument in all that he has done in the extension of the church (verse 19) by *word and deed* (verse 18). Jesus sent his disciples 'to proclaim the kingdom of God and to heal' (Luke 9: 2) and we find that the leaders of the early church both performed miracles and preached. When Peter and John were one day going to the temple in Jerusalem they found a cripple lying at its gate, they healed him and then preached to the crowd that gathered (Acts 3). Here is *deed*, i.e. *miraculous sign*, and *word*: with the latter we associate *the power of the Holy Spirit* (cf. 15: 13). In Old Testament days God's *Spirit* gave men power to do mighty deeds; Paul believes that God's *Spirit* has the *power* to change men's lives ('the new path of life', 6: 4) when they respond in faith to the preaching of the Gospel.

Paul has carried out this preaching in all the area of the north-eastern Mediterranean seaboard; *Illyricum* was the Roman province on the eastern side of the Adriatic Sea. Paul does not mean that every Gentile in this highly populated area has heard about Jesus, but only that he has founded churches in all its great cities; now as he goes further afield these are left to spread themselves.

20–1. Paul believed that it was the function of an apostle to lay the *foundations* of churches (cf. on 1: 1) and he is driven on by this to go to fresh areas. Others will build on the foundations he has laid, but he will not build on the foundations of others. There is nothing in the passage to imply that Rome was *another man's foundation* (cf. pp. 5 f.); he is only explaining why he is moving to Spain (15: 23) from an area which he regards as fully covered (verse 19). In so doing he is fulfilling a prophecy of Scripture (Isa. 52: 15, from the Septuagint, where the application to Jesus may be made more easily than in the Hebrew). ✳

PAUL'S FUTURE PLANS

22 That is why I have been prevented all this time from com-
23 ing to you. But now I have no further scope in these parts,
24 and I have been longing for many years to visit you on my way to Spain; for I hope to see you as I travel through, and to be sent there with your support after having enjoyed
25 your company for a while. But at the moment I am on my
26 way to Jerusalem, on an errand to God's people there. For Macedonia and Achaia have resolved to raise a common

fund for the benefit of the poor among God's people at
Jerusalem. They have resolved to do so, and indeed they 27
are under an obligation to them. For if the Jewish Christians shared their spiritual treasures with the Gentiles, the
Gentiles have a clear duty to contribute to their material
needs. So when I have finished this business and delivered 28
the proceeds under my own seal, I shall set out for Spain by
way of your city, and I am sure that when I arrive I shall 29
come to you with a full measure of the blessing of Christ.

I implore you by our Lord Jesus Christ and by the love 30
that the Spirit inspires, be my allies in the fight; pray to God
for me that I may be saved from unbelievers in Judaea and 31
that my errand to Jerusalem may find acceptance with
God's people, so that by his will I may come to you in a 32
happy frame of mind and enjoy a time of rest with you.
The God of peace be with you all. Amen.   33

✻ Paul tells them his travel plans. First to go to Jerusalem with
money that has been gathered for the poor of the church there;
then to pay a short visit to Rome; from there to go on to a fresh
area of mission work, Spain. He desires their help in prayer for
all this.

22–4. Paul has *been prevented* from *coming* earlier to the capital
of the Empire by his activity east of Rome; this is now complete so far as the work of an apostle is concerned (see on 15:
17–19). However, the purpose of his proposed *visit* to Rome is
not to work there (cf. verses 20–1) but to go beyond it to *Spain*.
We do not know why Paul chose Spain rather than N. Africa or
Gaul (France) as the next area to evangelize. It may be because
Spain had many trading connexions with the East and there
were a number of synagogues in it; when Paul came to a new
town he was accustomed to begin his work in the Jewish synagogue (cf. p. 4 and note on 1: 16). When he goes on to Spain
he hopes he will have the *support* of the Roman church. He

probably expects letters of introduction to people in Spain, money to assist his travelling and leave him free to preach, and perhaps someone to accompany him—Paul rarely travelled alone on his missionary work. His visit to Rome will not be prolonged (*for a while*); he will certainly preach the Gospel to them (1: 15), but this does not conflict with the principle of 15: 20–1, since he will not be staying in Rome nor coming primarily to evangelize.

25–7. Before Paul comes to Rome he has to go to *Jerusalem* (cf. p. 6) to pay an *obligation*. The *Gentile* Christians of the churches he has founded are Christians only because the *Jewish Christians* were such first (cf. chapters 9–11); from the latter they received the *spiritual treasures* of the Gospel; the Gentile Christians cannot return these treasures but they can share their *material* possessions. So in *Macedonia* and *Achaia* (parts of modern Greece) they have very willingly raised money for *the poor* of the Christian church (*God's people*) in *Jerusalem*. From the very earliest days the Jerusalem church was troubled with poverty (cf. Acts 6); many who had property sold it to try and alleviate the situation (Acts 4: 34–7); this could be only a temporary palliative and once the money was exhausted there was nothing more to fall back on. Paul encouraged his Gentile churches to act to meet this need because it also helped to hold together the Jewish and Gentile sections of the church.

28–9. When Paul has personally and safely *delivered* this confirmation of the Gentiles' love he will start out for Rome and *Spain*. He believes this is God's plan. Thus the *blessing of Christ* will be on his travel arrangements, and he will also bring a *blessing* from *Christ* to the Christians at Rome. His letter to them with its instruction and help is already such a blessing and what he brings will continue the blessing (cf. 1: 11).

30–2. Paul brings them 'the blessing of Christ' (verse 29), but he also seeks their help, for they and he serve a common *Lord* (*our* Lord) and both are *inspired* by the *love* that the *Spirit* gives (cf. 5: 5). Their prayers for his journey to Jerusalem will assist him because it may be dangerous and difficult. He may suffer persecution from unbelievers, i.e., the Jews (this actually happened: Acts 21: 27 — 25: 12); or he may find the more Jewish section of the church in Jerusalem (*God's people*) suspicious of the gift he is bringing and unwilling to receive it because they are not completely reconciled to the idea that Gentiles are their equals within the church (cf. pp. 2–3). If through the help of their prayers these two difficulties are overcome, it will mean that he will *come* to Rome in a *happy frame of mind*, and that in Rome he will be consoled and refreshed by their 'encouragement' (1: 12); *rest* does not mean relaxation.

33. He has desired that they should pray for *peace* on his journey and it is this same *peace* that he prays they will be allowed to enjoy through his presence with them. ✻

GREETINGS

I commend to you Phoebe, a fellow-Christian who holds **16** office in the congregation at Cenchreae. Give her, in the 2 fellowship of Christ, a welcome worthy of God's people, and stand by her in any business in which she may need your help, for she has herself been a good friend to many, including myself.

Give my greetings to Prisca and Aquila, my fellow- 3 workers in Christ. They risked their necks to save my 4 life, and not I alone but all the gentile congregations are grateful to them. Greet also the congregation at their 5 house.

Give my greetings to my dear friend Epaenetus, the first convert to Christ in Asia, and to Mary, who toiled hard for 6 you. Greet Andronicus and Junias my fellow-countrymen 7 and comrades in captivity. They are eminent among the apostles, and they were Christians before I was.

Greetings to Ampliatus, my dear friend in the fellow- 8 ship of the Lord, to Urban my comrade in Christ, and to 9

10 my dear Stachys. My greetings to Apelles, well proved in
11 Christ's service, to the household of Aristobulus, and my
countryman Herodion, and to those of the household of
12 Narcissus who are in the Lord's fellowship. Greet Try-
phaena and Tryphosa, who toil in the Lord's service, and
13 dear Persis who has toiled in his service so long. Give my
greetings to Rufus, an outstanding follower of the Lord,
14 and to his mother, whom I call mother too. Greet Asyn-
critus, Phlegon, Hermes, Patrobas, Hermas, and all friends
15 in their company. Greet Philologus and Julia, Nereus and
his sister, and Olympas, and all God's people associated
with them.

16   Greet one another with the kiss of peace. All Christ's
congregations send you their greetings.

17   I implore you, my friends, keep your eye on those who
stir up quarrels and lead others astray, contrary to the
18 teaching you received. Avoid them, for such people are
servants not of Christ our Lord but of their own appetites,
and they seduce the minds of innocent people with smooth
19 and specious words. The fame of your obedience has
spread everywhere. This makes me happy about you; yet
I should wish you to be experts in goodness but simpletons
20 in evil; and the God of peace will soon crush Satan beneath
your feet. The grace of our Lord Jesus be with you!

21   Greetings to you from my colleague Timothy, and
from Lucius, Jason, and Sosipater my fellow-countrymen.
22 (I Tertius, who took this letter down, add my Christian
23 greetings.) Greetings also from Gaius, my host and host of
the whole congregation, and from Erastus, treasurer of this
city, and our brother Quartus.

✻ Paul greets various members of the church by name; he has
either known them previously or heard of them. He adds a
warning against false teachers (verses 17–20).

A problem exists here about the original form of the letter.
The doxology (the ascription of praise to God), 16: 25–7,
appears at different places in different manuscripts; some have
it after 14: 23, one (an early manuscript) after 15: 33, but the
majority of the more reliable have it as in the N.E.B.; a few
omit it altogether. Further uncertainty arises because the
blessing (16: 20) also appears in different positions. A second-
century heretical Christian, Marcion, put out an edition of the
letter with many variations including the omission of chapters
15 and 16; this accounts for the appearance of the doxology
after 14: 23. But since it also appears after 15: 33 we have to
ask, was there once an edition of the letter that ended at 15: 33?
If so, 1: 1 — 15: 33 would have been Paul's original letter to
Rome, and after writing it he decided to make a copy of it (because it was a careful and balanced statement of his views; cf.
pp. 7–8); he sent the copy to another church, probably that at
Ephesus, and added chapter 16 to it. This view has support in
the omission by a few manuscripts of the name Rome in 1:
7, 15, implying that there may have been copies in which there
was no mention of Rome. Moreover, Paul greets in chapter 16
a surprisingly large number of people (at least twenty-seven)
for a church which he had never visited and few of whose members he can have known. There was, of course, constant travel
between Rome and other cities; Paul may have known the
Christians he names before they went to Rome, and greets
them because he wishes to bring out every contact between
himself and Rome. But the warnings which he issues in 16:
17–20 are unlike those in other parts of the letter and would be
more appropriate to the situation in Ephesus than in Rome. We
shall examine these matters as we go through the chapter but
the balance of the argument would indicate that chapter 16 was
not written to Rome.

1–2. It is very likely that *Phoebe* conveyed Paul's letter to

Ephesus (or to Rome, see just above). We do not know the nature of her *office* in the congregation at *Cenchreae* (not far from Corinth, from where Paul was writing). The word Paul uses to describe her activity is from the same root as 'administration' in 12: 7. She has helped Paul and others in unspecified ways; Paul encourages his readers to help her. By such mutual help *fellow-Christians* express *the fellowship of Christ*.

3–5. *Prisca and Aquila*, wife and husband, forced to leave Rome (see p. 5), had met Paul in Corinth and gone with him to Ephesus (Acts 18: 2, 18, 26), where apparently they remained. *Prisca* is the diminutive of Priscilla, the name by which she is known in Acts. Once, in conditions unknown to us, they had *risked their necks* for Paul; since he refers to the thankfulness of the *gentile congregations* the danger may well have come from Jews. A later writing (2 Tim. 4: 19) again shows Prisca and Aquila at Ephesus. This favours the idea that chapter 16 was written to the church in that city. But there is no real reason why they may not have been to Rome in the interval, especially if they had business interests there. Whichever it was, a group of Christians met *at their house* for worship and fellowship. During the first two centuries there were no special church buildings, and the larger rooms in the houses of wealthy Christians were used for services and meetings. It is interesting that the first two people whom Paul names as active in the service of the church are women, Phoebe and *Prisca*.

5–7. *Epaenetus* was the *first convert* in the Roman province of Asia (lying in Western Turkey) of which Ephesus was the capital. If Paul was writing to Ephesus it would be natural to mention this fact about him; he does exactly this in writing to Corinth about Stephanas (1 Cor. 16: 15). But Epaenetus could have moved to Rome. *Mary*, a Jewish name, was another woman engaged in the work of the church. *Andronicus and Junias* were also Jews who had been converted in the very early days of the church before Paul had become a Christian. They were famous missionaries (this is the meaning here of *apostle*: see on 1: 1) and had suffered all the rigours of that life. Some manuscripts give a feminine form to *Junias*; she would then have been the wife of *Andronicus*.

8–15. Paul greets a large number of friends and fellow-workers—they are just so many names to us; he often qualifies the names with descriptive phrases which show that he knew them well. The names are those used mainly by slaves and freedmen, i.e. slaves who had been given, or who had purchased, their freedom. In form they are Jewish (e.g. *Herodion*), Greek (e.g. *Stachys, Hermes, Nereus*), and Latin (e.g. *Urban, Rufus, Julia*). They include the names of both men and women. The names are nearly all well known to us from surviving inscriptions and literature, and are common enough to have been found in any large city of the period. There is nothing which particularly associates them with Ephesus. Some may possibly be connected with Rome. Mark in his Gospel, written at Rome, calls the man who helped to carry Jesus' cross 'the father of Alexander and Rufus' (Mark 15: 21); he would hardly have mentioned Rufus unless he was someone known to the Christians in Rome. If the *Rufus* of 16: 13 is the same person, then Rom. 16 probably was written to Rome. There were several Jewish princes called *Aristobulus*, at least one of whom had lived in Rome just prior to our period; his *household* might still be there and one of its members might have been called *Herodion*, which was a common name in the family in other forms (cf. Herod, Herodias). However, such connexions to Rome through names are tenuous, since the names concerned are so common.

16. At one point in the worship of the early church, members gave *the kiss of peace* to those beside them; that Paul refers to this in the letter may indicate that it was to be read at a service of worship in which the *kiss* was given. Paul has been in touch with many of the *congregations* in regard to the collection for the church in Jerusalem (cf. p. 6 and 15: 26–9) and so he feels he can add their greetings to his own.

17–20. There is a sudden change of tone. The church is troubled by some who *with smooth and specious words stir up quarrels and lead* believers *astray*. It is difficult for us to identify them because Paul does not describe them in detail; he says only that they are *servants of their own appetites*. His readers must have known whom he intended. He speaks so harshly about them that they cannot be identified with either of the groups described in 14: 1 — 15: 13. *appetites* (the lower instincts) implies immoral behaviour on their part; they cannot therefore have been those who wished to impose the Jewish law on Gentile Christians (see pp. 2–3). By the beginning of the second century there were groups claiming to be Christian and generally termed Gnostic; some of them taught that provided a man knew ('Gnostic' comes from the Greek word for knowledge) and believed the correct doctrine, it did not matter what he did with his body, i.e. he could follow his *appetites* as much as he liked. Paul is probably attacking here what crystallized out later into this movement; we find him opposing similar immoral tendencies in other letters, e.g. 1 Cor. 6: 12–20. The gnostic movement was strong in the area of Ephesus much earlier than in Rome. That its beliefs are not mentioned before in the letter would confirm the argument that chapter 16 was not written to Rome. If, however, it was, we must assume that just before he finished the letter Paul had received new information about danger to the church there and now refers to it.

the teaching you received: Paul is not referring to the teaching in his letter but to the common fund of Christian instruction on which we have seen him draw several times (1: 3–4; 4: 24–5; 6: 3, 17; 10: 9–10; 12: 9–21; cf. 15: 14).

The fame of your obedience: see on 1: 8.

the God of peace: i.e. the God who creates peace and overcomes *quarrels* and divisions.

crush Satan: this goes back to Gen. 3: 15 where it is promised that Eve's seed (taken by the early church to be Jesus) will bruise the serpent (taken by the early church to be *Satan*, a name given by the Jews to the devil): this will take place when the world ends, which as we have seen Paul expects soon (cf. on 11: 30–1; 13: 11). In that time there will be real and lasting *peace*.

The grace of our Lord Jesus be with you: Paul elsewhere puts such blessings at the very end of his letters. Some manuscripts put this after 16: 23 (as verse 24) and others after 16: 27; the better ones have it here. It is easy to see that a copyist might transfer it to the more normal position. Paul probably feels it appropriate here after the harsh words of verses 16–20.

21–3. Greetings from those with Paul. *Timothy* frequently accompanied Paul and undertook special work for him. *Lucius, Jason and Sosipater* may have been delegates of the congregations contributing to the collection who were now with Paul (see p. 6 and 15:25–9). Men with the same names are mentioned in Acts 13: 1; 17: 5–9, but we cannot be sure they are the same people. Paul usually dictated his letters and *Tertius*, his secretary, here adds his own greeting: he was probably known personally to the readers. Paul was staying in Corinth with *Gaius*, who was well-to-do and ready to entertain every Christian who came to him. *Erastus* was a prominent civic official. ✻

PRAISE TO GOD

To him who has power to make your standing sure, 25 according to the Gospel I brought you and the proclamation of Jesus Christ, according to the revelation of that divine secret kept in silence for long ages but now disclosed, 26 and through prophetic scriptures by eternal God's command made known to all nations, to bring them to faith and obedience—to God who alone is wise, through Jesus 27 Christ, be glory for endless ages! Amen.

✻ In a single complex sentence God is praised for all he has done in making salvation known through Jesus.

Paul quite often places doxologies like this at suitable points in the course of his argument (e.g. 11: 33–6), but never elsewhere does he end a letter with one. We would expect that a doxology would sum up the reasons for praise of God in the preceding argument but there is no reference to the *revelation* of the *divine secret* elsewhere in this letter. There are also differences of language and style from Paul's normal usage. For these reasons it is probable that Paul did not write this doxology but that someone else added it afterwards.

25–7. *him*, i.e. God. He alone *has power* to protect and preserve the church within the Christian faith (cf. 1: 11). That God can do this is known from the Gospel Paul has preached; *I brought you*, however, is a mistranslation; the same phrase is rendered, 'So my gospel declares' in 2: 16. Paul has not yet been to Rome and cannot therefore be made to say that he has brought the Gospel there. His Gospel, as for example we have it in this letter, is a *proclamation of Jesus Christ*. From the beginning of time this had been kept *secret* but is *now disclosed*—in the fact of Jesus' life, death and resurrection and in the proclamation of those events. The *prophetic scriptures* are those of the Old Testament on which the early Christians continually drew to prove that their preaching of Jesus was true and that it was intended not for Jews only but for *all nations*. All that God has done *through Jesus Christ* shows that he *alone is wise;* so *glory* should be ascribed to him alone.

✻　✻　✻　✻　✻　✻　✻　✻　✻　✻　✻　✻　✻

Let us look back over the way we have come through the letter. After introducing himself, Paul announces that his subject is the way in which God rights wrong and brings life to men (1: 16–17). The wrong that requires righting is the wrong that is in men. Paul shows that both Gentiles—those who have no special knowledge of God—and Jews—those who are God's people and therefore have such a special knowledge—have been 'wrong' within themselves, i.e. sinful. Left to themselves they are not able to put that wrong right. Their attempt to live by their own understanding of what God requires, i.e. his law, never succeeds; in fact it only serves to lead them further away from him (1: 18 — 3: 20).

However God himself has worked out a way by which the wrong in men may be righted; this has involved the death of his son Jesus; those who respond by faith to what God has done find that they are no longer in the wrong before God, but in the right, i.e., they are justified (3: 21 — 4: 25). The changed relationship in which they now stand to God works a change within themselves. This change is so great that a new humanity may be regarded as having begun with Jesus—a people with a new quality of life. It is for the very reason that they are different from what they were before that they can be summoned to dedicate themselves to God and to serve him; because they are changed people this is no longer a hopeless call (5: 1 — 7: 6). Yet they are not perfect and can easily slip back into doing wrong (7: 7–25). But God will not now condemn them; they have been put in the right and are living new lives. The nature of this new life is now explained in terms of God's Spirit who lives with them and works in their lives. Through this change in men God will eventually put right all the wrong in the universe (8: 1–39).

What is the relationship of the new humanity to the special people, the Jews, whom God chose for himself? This problem arises because the Jews do not allow themselves to be put in the right by God through Jesus. Because of their resistance to God they have lost their position. God will, however, eventually bring them back into the new humanity—the wrong within them will be put right. Jews and Gentiles will thus finally be one people. God continually works through the events of history— the choice of the Jews, the death and resurrection of Jesus, the conversion of the Gentiles—to gain this end (9: 1 — 11: 36).

The new humanity is called to serve God. Because it is new and not caught up in the old network of wrong, it is able to do so. In broad strokes Paul sets down the kind of life which those who belong to the new humanity should live. As they do so, actual wrongs will disappear out of their lives and actual rightness or goodness will appear. The source and motive of this goodness is love to all men (12: 1 — 15: 13).

Paul ends by outlining his future movements and his hope of coming to Rome on his way to take the good news of Jesus to Spain.

FURTHER READING

Books on the Letter to the Romans

A. M. Hunter, *The Epistle to the Romans* (S.C.M. Torch Bible Commentaries).

F. F. Bruce, *Romans* (Tyndale).

K. E. Kirk, *Romans* (Clarendon Bible, O.U.P.).

More advanced books

C. K. Barrett, *A Commentary on the Epistle to the Romans* (A. & C. Black).

C. H. Dodd, *The Epistle to the Romans* (Hodder; Fontana).

F. J. Leenhardt, *The Epistle to the Romans* (Lutterworth).

Books on Paul

C. H. Dodd, *The Meaning of Paul for Today* (Hodder; Fontana).

A. M. Hunter, *Interpreting Paul's Gospel* (S.C.M.).

M. Dibelius and W. G. Kümmel, *Paul* (Longmans).

A. D. Nock, *St Paul* (Home University Library).

J. S. Stewart, *A Man in Christ* (Hodder).

More advanced books on the thought of Paul

C. A. Scott, *Christianity According to St Paul* (C.U.P.).

D. E. H. Whiteley, *The Theology of St Paul* (Blackwell).

T. W. Manson, *On Paul and John* (Studies in Biblical Theology No. 38, S.C.M.).

INDEX